THE FUNDING PROCESS:

Grantsmanship and Proposal Development

by
VIRGINIA A. DECKER
and
LARRY E. DECKER

THE FUNDING PROCESS:

Grantsmanship and Proposal Development

By Virginia A. Decker & Larry E. Decker

Published by

Cover Design
Creative Cartoon Co.
Charlottesville, Va.

Community Collaborators
P. O. Box 5429
Charlottesville, Va. 22903

Typesetting
Fred Heblich
Charlottesville, Va.

International Standard Book Number: 0-930388-02-X
Library of Congress Catalog Card Number: 77-92892

Single copy, $6.95

THE DYNAMIC PROCESS

Citizenship and Progress Development

by Virginia A. Decker & Larry E. Decker

Published

Cover Design   Community Collaborators   Typesetting
Creative Cartoon Co.   P. O. Box 5429   Birch Booklet
Charlottesville, Va.   Charlottesville, Va. 22905   Charlottesville, Va.

International Standard Book Number: 0-930388-02-X
Library of Congress Catalog Card Number: 77-92862

Single copy $6.95

ACKNOWLEDGEMENTS

Just as the successful completion of the grantsmanship process is often the result of team efforts, so too, is this book the result of team efforts and influences which go far beyond the obvious ones which exist between husband and wife. In our years of experience with the funding process, many individuals and organizations have contributed to, influenced, and enhanced our grantsmanship skills and expertise. We wish we could acknowledge everyone, but that is impossible because the team roster contains too many names. However, several individual acknowledgements must be made because to each we owe a special thank you.

We wish to express our sincere appreciation:

- To the professional colleagues and associates of the Lane County Youth Project who were part of a valuable learning experience which resulted from addressing ambitious goals and charting innovative directions funded by federal grants from H.E.W., Office of Juvenile Delinquency and Youth Development, and Office of Economic Opportunity.

- To the University of Oregon as the institution which provided the exposure to the world of soft money and the institutional complexities of the grantsmanship process; and in particular, to Larry L. Neal, the writer of the Higher Education Act Title I grant that established the Center for Leisure Studies and Community Service, and to Mary Jo Hall, Director of the Office of Federal Relations, who was of immeasurable assistance in de-mystifying the complexities of securing funds from federal sources.

- To the staff and Board of Directors of the Charles Stewart Mott Foundation who have provided valuable support, advice, and encouragement over a long period of time and in a variety of situations.

- To Sherry P. Lancaster whose initial request to help with a series of grant and proposal writing workshops for the Virginia State Agency for Title I of the Higher Education Act created the need

5

to conceptualize concretely the funding process and whose initial prodding to develop workshop materials began the writing process which eventually resulted in this grantsmanship book.

To these people we are especially indebted. But again, to all those individuals engaged in funded projects and associated with funding sources coast-to-coast who have directly or indirectly contributed to our grantsmanship efforts, we want to say thank you.

Virginia and Larry
Charlottesville, Va.
January, 1978

Table of Contents

INTRODUCTION

Grantsmanship

Grantsmanship is a term commonly used by both individuals and institutions to refer to the process of seeking external funding. In definitive terms, grantsmanship is an organized way of seeking funds from an external funding source to support a desired activity. Securing funds from a funding source to undertake or maintain programs, projects, or research has become a fact of life for many institutions and individuals. Almost half a million United States institutions are supported wholly or partially by grant-making organizations, and the number of individuals, students and scholars receiving some form of grant is even greater.

Grant-making organizations are numerous. The 1975 *Catalog of Federal Domestic Assistance* listed more than 1,000 programs administered by 60 different federal departments, agencies, commissions and councils. It is estimated that 25,000 foundations will confer some 400,000 grants each year.[1] Because business and industrial corporations make grants in different ways, it is difficult to project a realistic estimate of corporate grant-making. Estimates have been made, however, which suggest approximately $1 billion is awarded annually in grants and contracts outside the industrial sector's research and development programs.[2]

The competition for funds is intense. Grant monies in both the public and private sectors are decreasing while the number of people applying for them is increasing. One source estimated that more than 95 out of every 100 applicants will have their proposals turned down.[3] Another source stated that "only about 50 to 60 percent of

---

[1] Howard Hillman and Karin Abarbanel, *The Art of Winning Foundation Grants* (New York: The Vanguard Press, Inc., 1975), p. 15.

[2] Virginia White, *Grants, How To Find Out About Them and What To Do Next* (New York: Plenum Press, 1975), p. vii.

[3] Hillman and Abarbanel, *Art of Winning Foundation Grants*, p. 15.

applications to the National Institute of Health are now approved by the reviewing committees, and these applications must then survive a strict priority valuation before actually being funded."[4]

Thus, developing grantsmanship skills is becoming a necessity for many institutions and individuals if they are to compete successfully for the funds which they need to carry out desired activities. Grantsmanship is now being considered an "art" as well as a knowledge base.

The "Art" of Grantsmanship

Grantsmanship is a process that can be identified by distinct phases of activity. Although referred to by various terms, the phases involve the sequential activities of:

a. developing an idea
b. organizing for action
c. establishing contact with a funding source
d. writing a proposal and following up
e. administering the grant

Because of the stiff competition for funds, however, today's successful grantsmen must do more than just complete the process. They must be competent in their fields of specialization and skilled in identifying the most likely sources of funding. Careful attention to details concerning the phases of grantsmanship as well as details in planning, organizing, and carrying out activities, both within the institution and without, is an important aspect. In addition, they must master the "art" of making their presentations and proposals stand out from those of all other applicants to the funding source.

Using the term "art" to identify the less tangible qualities of grantsmanship does not mean that these are not acquired qualities. To try to determine just what qualities comprise the "art," a consensus of opinions of professionals in the field was sought. In addition to experience, the seven most mentioned qualities were:

---

[4]Lois DeBakey, "The Persuasive Proposal," *Foundation News,* July, August, 1977, p. 20.

salesmanship, communication skills, administrative skills, good human relations, persistence, and dedication.[5]

The Grantsman

The discussions in the following sections refer in a rather impersonal way to "the grantsman." Who is the grantsman? Is the grantsman in one section the same as the grantsman in another section? These are both logical questions to ask.

The term "grantsman" is used to indicate the person carrying out the specific activities being discussed at a particular point in the grantsmanship process. This type of reference is used to simplify the discussion. In many cases, the tasks will be undertaken by more than one person and there will not be an identifiable grantsman. Because of the range of activities and the variety of skills and expertise involved in the grantsmanship process, the successful receipt of a grant often must be credited to more than one person.

Using this impersonal type of reference is not to imply that the grantsman cannot be one individual. However, one individual carrying out the entire range of grantsmanship activities is seldom the case. Usually the receipt of a grant results from the coordinated efforts of several individuals acting as a team and pooling their various skills, expertise, and knowledge.

[5]Hillman and Abarbanel, *The Art of Winning Foundation Grants*, p. 16.

Chapter One
PRE-PROPOSAL PHASE

The Environment

A grantsman does not exist in a vacuum, but functions in a particular environment and is almost always a member of an institution or organization. Occasionally grants are made to individuals but they are most often made to an institution. It is a fact that grant-makers are not likely to award funds to an individual who is not connected with a formal organization, usually a non-profit organization.

Awarding grants to institutions rather than to individuals has been the governmental policy for a long time. The terms of the 1969 Tax Reform Act have made it the policy of foundations as well. By law, foundations may fund only certain types of activities and the Act holds grant-makers responsible for seeing that no monies given by them are misused. Thus, although in theory they can fund individuals, "in practice, foundations give virtually all their money to organizations with IRS tax exempt status."[1]

The Individual Institutional Partnership

Just as the grantsman does not exist in a vacuum, neither does the institution. Each institution has a reason for being—a mission to be achieved. Institutional activities and projects are directed toward fulfillment of that mission, and the individuals who make up the institution have functions that assist in accomplishing it.

Generally, these individuals may be categorized into three groups: (a) the policy makers who provide basic direction for establishing the overall mission and direction, (b) the performers of the institution's primary functions, 'and (c) the administrators who have supporting functions. These three groups must work together in the generation of ideas that culminate in projects and activities if the

---

[1]Hillman and Abarbanel, *The Art of Winning Foundation Grants,* p. 20.

institution is to accomplish its mission. It is "the partnership between these three groups that can and must create an atmosphere conducive to the germination and expression of ideas."[2]

The creation of this atmosphere is important because ideas are essential to an institution. Every successful project or activity is based on a good idea. Without a climate which enhances institutional morale and encourages initiative coupled with organizational support for worthwhile ideas, there is little likelihood of generating the flow of ideas necessary for a healthy institution.

Idea Generation

The grantsmanship process begins with an idea for a project or activity that cannot be undertaken without securing funds from outside the institution. The idea usually will be generated by an individual either in response to a problem perceived in the environment or a need within a specific discipline or field of knowledge, or in response to appeals from some source for a solution to a problem which has already been identified. The idea will be formulated from the individual's assessment of the problem and will contain an indication of an approach to solving that problem. Regardless of the way in which it is generated, it is not likely that the idea will emerge fully developed.

Idea generation can be likened to the process of creating a sculpture from a piece of stone. The stone must be examined prior to chiseling the main features, adding the details, and polishing the final figure. *The Handbook of Grants and Contracts for Non-Profit Organizations*[3] presented a series of questions which should be answered by the originator of an idea in the process of formulating an idea. The questioning begins with the examination of the problem and the determination of what is to be solved.

1. What are you trying to solve?
2. What is the purpose of solving it?

―――――――――

[2]Jane C. Belcher and Julia M. Jacobsen, *A Process for the Development of Ideas* (Washington, D. C.: Government Relations Office, 1976), p. 1.

[3]William Willner and John P. Nichols, *Handbook of Grants and Contracts for Non-Profit Organizations* (Woodward, Oklahoma: Bethesda Research Institute, 1976), pp. 112-113.

3. Whom are you trying to help? Do they want it?
4. Who else has done it? What have you heard or read about it?
5. Why do you want to solve it?
6. Is it worth the time and money?

When the orginator has progressed to this point in formulating an idea, the individual will have decided if the idea is worth further exploration. If so, the goals and objectives begin to emerge.

1. What do you want to accomplish?
2. What other approaches or alternatives have you considered?
3. What effect on the problems will your idea have?
4. What other effects will the idea have?

At this point, the orginator should again evaluate the merits of the idea. If the idea continues to appear worthwhile, possible procedures should be examined.

1. What are you going to do?
2. How are you going to do it? With what and/or to whom are you going to do it?
3. Can you determine a strategy? What will you describe and how will you describe it?
4. What has to occur before you know you have done your job?
5. Can you determine the results?
6. What will happen if the results are unfavorable or inconclusive?

At this point in formulating the idea, the originator must begin to think in terms of personnel and resources.

1. Who is going to do what?
2. Are they qualified to do it?
3. What do they need to do it?
4. Will they be willing to do it?
5. Who else is likely to be involved and how?
6. Where will you do it?
7. What kinds of resources will you need?

When these questions have been answered to the individual's satisfaction and abilities, the originator is ready to share the idea with others. The idea must be shared because any new project or activity involves changes which can lead to adjustments, realignments, and sometimes compromises in the institution's priorities.

Preliminary Checking

Because the individual is part of the institutional partnership, those most likely to be affected by the idea should be consulted. Management experts agree that policy planning is a continuous process and that the relationship of an institution's projects and activities to its goals and objectives should be continually identified.[4] Thus, preliminary checking procedures are necessary to maintain institutional coordination.

The first people with whom the idea is likely to be shared are professional colleagues. If the idea is favorably received, it is then usually described to the Department Chairperson or Supervisor and others who might be directly or indirectly affected or involved with the future project. The preliminary checking is part of the communication and coordination which are essential to the successful development of the idea. This initial consultation will determine:

1. If the idea duplicates or conflicts with any other project or activity,
2. If the project is acceptable in terms of the institution's goals and objectives, and
3. What, if any, resources and facilities are available.

If the idea continues to be promising, it must be shared with all those whom it will affect. If the originator of the idea will not be the Project Director, that individual should be identified as soon as possible and brought into the developmental process. Evidence shows that the closeness and/or directness of the Project Director's relationship to the institution is a fundamental factor in the success

---

[4] Joseph Battle, C. Bruce Melville, Kenneth Connell, Donna Taffe and Ed Kramer, "How to Develop an Effective Fund-Raising Strategy," *Grantsmanship Center News* (August-October, 1976), p. 11.

or failure of the project.[5] The Project Director can function more effectively when this individual knows the amount and/or extent of resources, facilities, services, and personnel available for use; the agreed upon prerogatives and obligations; the proper administrative channels for maintaining coordination and communication; etc.

Idea Development

The sharing of the idea phase in the grantsmanship process cannot be treated lightly. It is not only essential to insure institutional cooperation and coordination, but it is also essential to the full development of an idea into a plan of action. The sharing must be a "giving and taking" of information on the part of all those affected by the project or activity as well as others who may have pertinent information or experience. J. M. Ziman underscored the value of sharing information in his reminder that,

> This technique, of soliciting many modes of contributions to the store of human knowledge, has been the secret of Western science since the seventeenth century, for it achieves a corporate, collective power that is far greater than any one individual can exert.[6]

As the idea is discussed, the goals, objectives, and general ramifications of the project or activity will gradually become more clearly understood. At this point in idea development, it is now possible to prepare an internal document for use by the institution's staff and board members. Its preparation initiates the process of writing the idea down on paper in concrete terms. The document should describe the proposed project or activity as clearly and concisely as possible with as many specifics as have been formulated in the idea sharing process. It should also relate the idea to the organization's long range plans. This internal document integrates the idea into:

a) The history and background of institutional growth and previous achievements.

b) A projection of institutional undertakings in coming years in terms of the institution's capabilities.

[5] White, *Grants,* p. 176.

[6] Marianna O. Lewis, ed., *The Foundation Directory* (New York: The Foundation Center, 1975), p. ix.

In the consultations that follow the presentation of this internal document, the idea will be carefully scrutinized, both in terms of its own feasibility and in terms of its desirability. In this process, institutional policies should be clarified on such matters as facility use, reimbursement of overhead costs, faculty and/or staff involvement, release time, equipment, property and material acquisitions, use of patents and copyrights, and any other factors relevant to specific aspects of activities of the proposed undertaking.

In the consultation process, the initial document will also be refined and modified. If the idea has received tentative approval, a concept paper of the proposed project or activity can be prepared. This document will be a refinement of the internal document and will contain the basic information necessary for continuing the grantsmanship process.

The concept paper is basically an outline of the proposed project or activity. It is composed of brief statements of:

—What is to be done.
—Why it is worth doing.
—What will be the specific objectives.
—Who is to do what.
—What facilities and/or other resources will be required.
—How long it will take.
—How much it is estimated to cost.

It is at the stage of writing the concept paper that the grantsmanship process begins to differ depending on the way the idea was generated. If it occurred in response to an appeal from some funding source for a solution to an already identified problem, the idea must be adjusted to conform to the guidelines specified by that funding source. If ·it occurred in response to an individual's assessment of a problem, the idea will be developed in terms of the institution's guidelines and criteria and a funding source will be subsequently sought. Even though the continuing sequence of activities will differ depending on how the idea was generated, it should be remembered that all funding sources will ask for basically the same information. This information is the same kind already gathered if the developmental process has been orderly, thoughtful and thorough.

When the information has been organized in the form of the concept paper, the grantsman is ready to begin the "organizing for action" phase of the grantsmanship process. This pre-application for funds phase encompasses the activities of the grantsman after the concept paper has been completed and before an application is made to a specific funding source. It consists of two simultaneous procedures:

1. Consultation with officials of the institution that will receive and administer the funds.
2. Consultation with representatives of the prospective funding source.

Chapter Two
ORGANIZING FOR ACTION

A Note of Caution

In the enthusiasm of pursuing and developing an idea, the grantsman may lose sight of an old adage, "You don't get something for nothing." In every grant agreement, regardless of the degree of formality of the negotiation process or of the terms of the receipt of funds, is implied the understanding that the grantee has the responsibility to perform activities which will fulfill expectations of the grantor. Every funding source views a proposed project or activity in the light of its own institutional mission and the possible effect on its goals and objectives. Thus, there must be a balance between the goals and objectives of the institution seeking funds and the goals and objectives of a possible source of funds. An inherent danger in seeking funds from a particular source is that the price may be too high. As William Brown, Commissioner of the Equal Employment Commission, stated, "There is a payment for any funds received and the price may be to turn you around and take on somebody else's agenda."[1]

Search for a Source of Funds

If the idea has been developed in line with the institution's guidelines and criteria, no specific source of funds will have been identified. The grantsman must now begin the process of identifying and researching possible funding sources. In this process, the grantsman identifies potential funding sources; secures information about them; and assesses the appropriateness of their goals, objectives, and guidelines to the idea and to the goals and objectives of the institution seeking the funds.

Basically, the sources of funds are: government, foundations,

---

[1]Battle, Melville, Connell, and Kramer, "How to Develop An Effective Fund Raising Strategy," *The Grantsmanship Center News,* pp. 8-9.

and private businesses and individuals. In terms of total funds granted, the government provides by far the largest amount whereas individuals provide a relatively insignificant amount. In searching for funds, however, no category should be overlooked.

Individuals and Businesses—The most difficult category to monitor is this private category. The individuals, corporations, and organizations who engage in philanthropy are difficult to identify. Usually they give funds to benefit a specific cause or a specific area, and with a few exceptions, are not widely known. Thus, knowledge of their philanthrophy may not be readily available. If the grantsman is fortunate enough to identify a source easily, it will usually be through personal knowledge, word of mouth, or media coverage.

Even when a private source is identified, receiving information about the conditions under which funds are granted can be difficult. Some contact must be made, usually in the form of a letter, telephone call, or personal visit. It is then up to the potential source whether or not the matter will be pursued further.

It should be noted that there have been some changes in this category of private funds. Because of the 1969 Tax Reform Act, some corporations no longer operate corporate foundations, but do continue to maintain active corporate grant programs. Their corporate contributions offices differ significantly from corporate foundations. They do not operate under the supervision of a Board of Directors and the level of contributions is totally dependent on the profit the corporation itself has made.[2]

Even though these potential sources of funds are much more difficult to identify than those in other categories, the time and trouble may be well rewarded. In 1974 corporations contributed $1.17 billion.[3]

Foundations—No one outside IRS knows exactly how many foundations exist, and even they may not have an accurate figure because there is some overlap in categories. Although estimates of the number range from 20,000 to 50,000, approximately 25,000 is

---

[2]Walker A. Williams and Company, Inc., *Resource Development in the Private Sector* (Washington, D. C.: Produced under contract administered by the American Revolution Bicentennial Administration, 1976), p. 6.

[3]*Ibid.*, p. 1.

the figure most often given. Of the thousands of foundations in existence, only about 200 to 300 are well-known.

The definition of a foundation is sometimes unclear because "the prestigeful name foundation has been adopted by many organizations which . . . have no proper right to its use."[4] These organizations "include agencies which solicit contributions instead of disbursing from an established fund and some which are trade associations, pressure groups or outright rackets."[5]

The 1969 Tax Reform Act attempted to establish a legal definition. It decreed [Section 501(c)(3)] that religious, educational, scientific, cultural, and charitable organizations are either private foundations or they are not; and it established the criteria to determine such classification.

There are three major categories of private foundations.

a) Community foundations are local organizations which receive bequests and contributions from donors in their locality and which administer those funds for the purposes designated by trustees and donors.

b) Corporate foundations are established and administered by corporations which contribute funds to them.

c) Family foundations are established with bequests and contributions of the family members and funds are administered for purposes determined by family members.[6]

Foundation grants are made for many purposes and range in size from millions of dollars to a hundred dollars. The 1973 Foundation Grants Index gave a breakdown in the most funded fields counting grants over $5,000. This breakdown provides an indication of the current funding interests even though the relative share of each field changes from year to year as the popularity or priority of the field changes. For example, education varied 34% to 41% over a ten year period.[7] The following shows the breakdown of

---

[4]*Ibid.*, p. 2.

[5]White, *Grants*, p. 119.

[6]Walker A. Williams and Company, Inc., *Resource Development in the Private Sector*, p. 2.

[7]Hillman & Abarbanel, *Art of Winning Foundation Grants*, p. 170.

the most funded fields and what percentage of the monies awarded to a major field went to particular subfields.

36% education
- 37% endowment
- 19% higher education
- 10% buildings and equipment

24% health
- 34% medical education
- 26% hospitals
- 15% public health
- 13% medical care and rehabilitation

12% science and technology
- 27% medical research
- 10% environmental studies
- 10% law

9% welfare
- 21% community development
- 21% youth agencies
- 13% child welfare
- 10% community funds

9% international activities
- 30% education
- 25% health and welfare
- 23% technical assistance
- 13% international studies

8% humanities
- 33% performing arts
- 28% museums
- 15% music

2% religion
- 41% theological education
- 27% religious welfare
- 17% religious associations[8]

---

[8] *Ibid.*

The total amount awarded by foundations is small in comparison to amounts awarded by government. But the amount is far from insignificant. A survey compiled in *Giving U. S. A.* reported that in 1974 foundations contributed $2.11 billion.[9]

Government—Changes have been taking place in the granting policies of government in the last few years, especially at the federal level. The grant-making boom of the 1960's is over; and policy guidelines, criteria, and procedures have become more definite and stringent. But of more importance to the grantsman is the change in the form of granting. The so-called New Federalism philosophy emphasizes strengthening the role of state and local governments in decision making and administering federally appropriated funds.

This decentralization of programs presents some additional difficulties in identifying sources of funds. It has added another layer of bureaucracy with which to become familiar. State and local agencies have established counterparts of the national agencies and of each other resulting in an overlap of federal, state, county, and municipal units.[10]

Another change in form is that an increasing amount of federally appropriated funds is being distributed through the contract process rather than through the grant process. (See Chapter Six for an explanation of the two processes.) The increased need for governmental agencies to be more accountable has led to many agencies desiring to maximize their degree of control. The contract process allows an agency to make sure its problems are addressed exactly as it thinks they should be. Compared to a grant, a contract's statement of work, the legally binding agreement as to what the contractor is to do, is longer and more detailed.[11] Further, if what is specified in the statement of work is not done, the government is not obligated to pay.

Another notable change is that increasing amounts of funds are becoming available for applied research as opposed to basic research.

---

[9]William A. Walker and Company, Inc., *Resource Development in the Private Sector,* p. 1.

[10]White, *Grants,* p. 42.

[11]Keith Baker, "The New Contractsmanship," *The Grantsmanship Center News* (March-April, 1976), p. 24.

Usually these funds are distributed through the contract process.[12] The energy crisis of the 1970's may well influence the grant-making priority areas of many governmental agencies in much the way Sputnik did in the 1950's and 1960's.

1he following National Science Foundation chart shows the influence of the energy crisis.[13] One-fourth of the increase in federal funds for research and development between 1974 and 1978 is in the field of energy.

Federal Funds for Research

Federal obligations in millions of dollars
Fiscal years

Estimated

Subject	1969	1970	1971	1972	1973	1974	1975	1976	1977	1978
National defense	$ 8,354	$ 7,976	$ 8,106	$ 8,898	$ 8,998	$ 8,975	$ 9,621	$10,346	$11,917	$12,907
Space	3,732	3,510	2,893	2,714	2,601	2,478	2,511	2,863	2,972	3,140
Energy development and conversion	328	317	324	383	442	605	1,110	1,388	2,390	2,798
Health	1,127	1,126	1,338	1,589	1,624	2,096	2,177	2,366	2,622	2,683
Environment	315	354	465	533	651	693	837	899	1,101	1,098
Science and technology base	513	525	524	601	605	695	782	839	953	1,060
Transportation and communications	458	590	779	615	630	703	641	636	769	805
Natural resources	201	238	326	354	341	341	445	489	547	610
Agricultural products	225	241	247	291	297	291	349	388	444	488
Education	155	147	186	191	214	173	149	142	284	269
Income security and social services	97	106	128	125	157	134	148	133	156	148
Area and community development, housing and public services	49	91	89	87	97	96	102	104	111	99
Economic growth and productivity	56	80	99	63	75	72	67	84	98	97
International cooperation and development	27	32	32	29	33	27	30	45	53	71
Crime prevention and control	5	9	10	25	35	36	46	36	49	44
Total	$15,641	$15,340	$15,545	$16,498	$16,800	$17,415	$19,013	$20,759	$24,465	$26,317

SOURCE: NATIONAL SCIENCE FOUNDATION

In searching for a source of funds among the many governmental agencies, the grantsman must have some knowledge of what has been called "governmentese." In the public sector, it is customary to refer to departments, agencies, and programs by their initials. This use of acronyms in referring to agencies and programs

---

[12]*Ibid.*, p. 21.

[13]"Fact File," *The Chronicle of Higher Education,* November 7, 1977, p. 14.

26

makes identification difficult for someone who is not familiar with them. An added problem with learning the vocabulary of acronyms is that it is constantly growing and changing. Each new program, government office, commission, etc. adds to the list. Thus, it is helpful if the grantsman knows which sectors of government are more concerned with grant making.

Sources of Information

For some grantsmen, their own institution may have one or more offices which provide assistance in identifying possible sources of funds. Various titles for this type of office include Office of Sponsored Programs, Federal Relations Office, Developmental Office, or Research Office. In addition to information on a wide range of funding sources, these offices may have information regarding individuals and businesses granting funds to a particular field or area which is not readily available elsewhere.

Many grantsmen do not have ready access to an office which monitors funding sources and have to do their own research. The principal reference volumes are commonly found on library shelves.

Catalogue of Federal Domestic Assistance, a federal publication, is a compendium of government funding programs indexed by subject and by agency.

Annual Register of Grant Support, published by Academic Media, tries to index all grant support programs of foundations, governmental agencies, and business and professional organizations and is annually revised.

United States Government Manual, an annual publication and the official handbook of the federal government, contains descriptions of all federal agencies. Descriptions of agencies having grant programs include addresses to which requests for information can be written. The 1973-1974 edition contained a "Guide to Government Information" which explained how to keep up with U. S. government publications and discussed other information sources.

The Foundation Directory, published by the Foundation Center, provides the most complete listing of foundations indexed by state.

In addition, the Foundation Center has three national reference centers in New York, Washington, D. C., and Chicago, as well as regional centers in many states (See Appendix A). These centers are open to the public without charge and contain reference books, reports, foundations' annual reports on film, and foundation IRS information returns.

There are several periodicals which often contain information on sources of funds. Among those frequently used are:

Chronicle of Higher Education gives foundation and federal grant news of interest to higher education institutions.

Commerce Business Daily, published daily by the U. S. Department of Commerce, announces the bidding opportunities (RFP's) of government agencies and programs; although published five days a week, Monday's issue contains the "Numbered Notes," a list of specific pieces of information dealing with grants and contracts announced throughout the week.

Federal Notes, published semi-monthly by the University of Southern California, highlights regulatory notes from the *Federal Register* and provides information on current legislation, program plans and upcoming programs of federal agencies.

Federal Register, published by the U. S. Government Printing Office, includes announcements of new grant programs or changes in current programs.

Foundation News, published by the Council on Foundations, Inc., has a centerfold, "Foundation Grants Index," which is a guide to current grant-making activity.

The Grantsmanship Center News, published by the Grantsmanship Center, gives information on both government and private sources.

The Public Information law, frequently called the Freedom of Information Act, requires each governmental agency at every level to give information and advice. Every federal agency making grants must announce its programs and respond to requests for information. Thus, in exploring governmental sources of funds, it is possible to write to a particular department or agency for information on its areas of interest, funding priorities, and any requests for proposals it may have. Many departments and agencies publish information and helpful brochures and guides.

The major grant-making department of the federal government is Health, Education and Welfare (HEW). Four of its divisions, Public Health Service (PHS), Office of Education (OE), Office of Human Development (OHD), and Social and Rehabilitation Services (SRS) make many of the grants to states and other governmental subdivisions as well as awarding funds directly to institutions.

Other governmental departments and agencies awarding funds through grants and contracts are:

Department of Agriculture (USDA)
Department of Commerce
    Economic Development Administration (EDA)
    National Oceania and Atmospheric Administration (NOAA)
Department of Defense (DOD)
    includes Army, Navy and Air Force
Department of Housing and Urban Development (HUD)
Department of Interior
    Bureau of Land Management (BLM)
    Office of Water Resources Research (OWRR)
    National Park Service (NPS)
    Bureau of Indian Affairs (BIA)
Department of Justice
    Law Enforcement Assistance Administration (LEAA)
    Law Enforcement Education Programs (LEEP)
Department of Labor
    Manpower Administration (MA)
    Comprehensive Employment and Training Act (CETA)
Department of State
    Bureau of Educational and Cultural Affairs
Department of Transportation
    University Research Program
    Urban Mass Transportation Authority (UMTA)
Other Independent Agencies

Energy Research and Development Administration (ERDA)
National Science Foundation (NSF)
National Aeronautics and Space Administration (NASA)
Environmental Protection Agency (EPA)
National Foundations on the Arts and Humanities
  National Endowment for the Arts (NEA)
  National Endowment for the Humanities (NEH)

The Federal Information Centers operated by the General Services Administration were established to disseminate information on all aspects of the federal government. Anyone can call, write or visit the Centers for information on programs and services. (See Appendix B.)

Other sources of assistance in identifying possible sources of funds are the commercial information services. These services, generally for a fee, offer to provide information on funding programs of private and governmental sources. However, the cost should be examined in terms of the services and information to be received because most of the information provided by the information services is derived from sources available to everyone, such as the *Federal Register*, current legislation action, The Foundation Center publications, newspapers and periodical literature on government and foundation activities and programs.

Among the better known information services are:

Taft Products Inc., 100 Vermont Ave., N.W., Washington, D. C., publishes the Taft Information System which contains information on foundations and is updated three times a year. It also publishes a monthly newsletter, *The Foundation Report,* and a hotline letter.

Foundation Research Inc., Detroit, Michigan, provides information on foundations by state and selected region of the state. It also lists foundation grants made to a given geographic area.

Funding Sources Clearinghouse, Inc., 116 Michigan Ave., Chicago, Illinois, uses a computer to match grant seekers with grant prospects. Their data are supposed to include all U. S. foundations, all federal grant-making agencies, and many corporations and associations making grants.

ORYX Press Grant Information System, East Edgemont

Avenue, Scottsdale, Arizona, provides information, indexed by grant name, sponsoring organization, and subject, on U. S. government agencies, state government research organizations, private foundations, associations and U. S. corporations.

A Basic Library

The results of a questionnaire mailed to 650 members of the National Council of University Research Administrators to determine the information sources frequently used and their relative usefulness provided the basis for the following recommendations. The recommended basic libraries take into consideration the size of the organization and cost.

Recommendation One is for the small research unit or sub-unit within a large institution. The suggested publications provide information on a wide variety of programs for a cost not exceeding $100 per year: *Federal Register* ($50), *Foundation Directory* ($30), *Catalog of Federal Domestic Assistance* ($17), *NIH Guide for Grants and Award Programs* (free), *NSF Bulletin* (free), *Foundation Newsletters and Annual Reports* (i.e., Ford, Carnegie, Rockefeller) (free), *Federal Agency Dicretories and Reports* (free). Total cost, $97.

Recommendation Two is for a research office that services a larger variety of programs but which has budget limitations on the purchase of publications of $400 annually: Recommendation One Publications ($97), *Chronicle of Higher Education* ($20), *Federal Notes* ($48), *Commerce Business Daily* ($75), *Annual Register of Grant Support* ($41), *U.S. Government Manual* ($6), *Higher Education and National Affairs* ($25), *SRA Journal* ($15), *Science and Government Report* ($65). Total cost, $392. [14]

It was noted that several publications, *Commercial Clearing House-College and University Reports*, *Guide to Federal Assistance to Education*, *Government R & D Reports*, and *Federal Research Report*, were omitted from the recommendations because their cost was higher and would raise the recommendation above the $400 limit.[15] (See Appendix C for acquisition addresses.)

---

[13]Kenneth L. Beasley, "Information Sources for Research Administration," *Journal of the Society of Research Administrators*, Vol. VIII, No. 2, Fall, 1976.

[15]*Ibid.*

Foundation 990 Annual Reports

The most up-to-date sources of information on foundations are the 990 AR's annual reports which the foundations are required to submit to the Internal Revenue Service. The foundations are also required to send the 990 form to the state in which it is located. A foundation's 990 provides information in 10 general categories including:

- The address of the foundation's principal office and the names and addresses of its managers.
- The balance sheet and the annual totals for gifts and contributions received, gross income and disbursements.
- The grants made or approved during the year including, for each grant, the amount and purpose, the name and address of the recipient and the relationship, if any, between the recipient and the foundation's managers or major contributors.

Although the 990 AR's contain valuable current information, the grantsman may experience difficulties in obtaining the reports. Problems arise because foundations do not always send the form to the state, the forms are sometimes unorganized and some states do not make the reports publicly available. The October-December, 1977 issue of the *Grantsmanship Center News* contains a chart listing, by state, the contact person and/or office, the type of contact and hours, and any restrictions on public use. [16]

The reports can also be obtained from the Internal Revenue Service Center, P. O. Box 187, Cornwells Heights, PA 19020. Aperture cards or paper photocopies of a foundation's 990 can be ordered for a small charge. The grantsman should provide the full name of the foundation, the city and state in which it is located, the year of the return desired and the foundation's Employer Identification Number, if possible.

---

[16] "State Government Sources of Foundation Information," *The Grantsmanship Center News,* Vol. 3, No. 6, October-December, 1977, pp. 45-50.

Chapter Three
RESEARCHING POTENTIAL FUNDING SOURCES

Necessary Information

Although the monitoring process includes the phases of identifying potential funding sources, securing information on each identified source and assessing the appropriateness of each to the proposed project or activity, the grantsman usually will begin the process with at least an intuitive assessment. The nature of the proposed project or activity together with the type and geographic location of the institution involved and the grantsman's overall knowledge of funding sources will influence the choice of the type of funding to be sought.

Generally, unless an individual or business is known to the grantsman, most of the research will be concentrated on foundation and/or governmental sources. The choice of where to begin researching may be dictated by the historical role of foundation funding versus governmental funding. In general, foundation giving is freer of restrictions. Foundations can use their funds as "venture capital" to support projects or activities that have a calculated risk inherent in them. Government, on the other hand, is usually less venturesome. Government funds are public monies and the use of them often entails restrictions. The funds also are likely to be allocated in some manner among priority areas as well as on a population or geographic basis.

Regardless of the funding source or how the information is obtained, the grantsman must secure at least a minimum amount of information on each potential source. This information includes the correct name and address of the potential source, areas of interests, funding priorities, the size of grants, restrictions if any, dates and terms of proposal submission, and the contact person or office. This information is necessary to assess adequately the general character of a potential source in order to determine its appropriateness to the idea under consideration.

The general character of a foundation is deduced from its history. The description or reference found in one information source should be checked with those found in other sources. This double checking will not only insure greater accuracy but also will provide additional details and information. The description of a foundation's grant making will provide a general indication of its range of interests, whether it is concerned with a specific geographic area, the type of institution to whom it makes its awards, and the range in grant size.

The general character of a governmental agency or program can often be determined from the law or act establishing it and from the regulations and guidelines under which it awards funds. These documents indicate the kinds of projects and activities that can be funded as well as the manner in which funds are awarded.

Once a preliminary list of potential funding sources has been compiled, the grantsman must research in depth the ones which seem most likely to be interested in the proposed idea. There are no hard and fast rules that guarantee successfully finding a source of funds. But there are general techniques used by most successful grantsmen.

One technique recommended as a way of beginning the in-depth research is to work in "a series of concentric circles—beginning locally and expanding nationally in direct proportion to the effectiveness, appeal and growth of the program."[1] Checking local foundations, corporations and/or local and state agencies has the advantage of increasing the likelihood of the grantsman being familiar with the character of a funding source and of the source being familiar with the grantsman's institution. The research must be conducted thoroughly and with care because although having accurate information is essential, it is often difficult to get.

In order to assess further the appropriateness of a funding source, the grantsman needs information regarding the following:

1. Whether the proposed idea fits within the basic philosophy of the source and its funding priorities.

2. Whether the proposed costs are within its giving range.

3. Whether it funds solely or jointly; and if jointly, with what

[1]Walker A. Williams and Company, Inc., *Resource Development in the Private Sector*, p. 17.

types of other institutions and what percentage of total funding it would consider.

4. Whether it would consider funding the entire project or only certain segments, i. e., staff, equipment, materials, participant costs, institutional overhead, fringe benefits.

5. Whether matching funds are required, and if so, what kind.

6. Whether funding is short or long term and whether grant renewal is possible.

7. Whether there is a funding cycle, and if so, the deadlines to be met for proposal submission.

8. Whether there are any restrictions or special requirements to which applicants or institutions must agree, i. e., policies, copyrights, patents, information dissemination, auditing procedures, reporting requirements.

9. Whether a draft of the proposal can be submitted for review prior to formal submission of the proposal.

10. Whether there are guidelines for proposal submission and required forms.

How this information is obtained will vary depending on the character of the funding source and the grantsman's ability to make contact with that source.

Personal Contact

If the grantsman or the institution is experienced in seeking external funds, it is likely that informal contacts exist with some potential funding sources. For example, previous contact may have resulted in an agreement with a source's personnel to be kept informed on funding possibilities. Some funding sources keep files on these contacts describing individuals and institutions, the type of projects in which the contact is interested, and the contact's qualifications. The source can then send out information when it has funds for a particular area.

In other cases, the grantsman or someone within the institution may know a person who has a linkage to a funding source and who can initiate a contact. This person may be able to call attention to the proposed idea and indicate that the grantsman will be making direct contact. This contact person may even be able to make an appointment to see one of the funding source's staff members.

If no linkages exist to a funding source, the grantsman can initiate the contact. When possible, it is preferable to telephone. A telephone call is an effective way to initiate contact because the correspondence loads of many funding sources are heavy and responses to written requests cannot be made quickly. A telephone call has the added advantage of allowing the caller to speak directly to a representative of the funding source to explain the nature of the proposed idea and to receive instant feedback. If the idea is favorably received, it may be feasible to set up an appointment to explore further the idea and its funding potential.

When it is possible to make an appointment to meet with a representative of a funding source, preparation for the meeting should begin immediately. No matter how easily or casually the meeting was arranged, the grantsman must remember that there is no such thing as an informal meeting. The purpose of the meeting is to exchange information, and thorough preparation increases the chance of interesting the funding source in the proposed idea.

When a meeting has been arranged it is recommended that one or two representatives of the institution attend the meeting, usually the project director and a knowledgeable staff or board member. Because the time allotted for the meeting is usually limited, an agenda should be prepared. Many of the questions asked by the funding source will be the same as those initially asked by the institution itself in the process of idea development. Only a few necessary materials, such as the concept paper and limited supporting documents and credentials, should be taken to the meeting. Thus, whoever attends the meeting should be thoroughly prepared to answer and ask questions. Edith Friedman, Executive Director of the Bruner Foundation, gave several conduct suggestions:

1. Be businesslike
2. Be honest
3. Know what you mean to do
4. Ask questions
5. And finally never, never argue about the relevance of the proposed project to the funding source's program[2]

---

[2]White, *Grants*, pp. 219-220.

The tone of the meeting will enhance the exchange of information. Careful attention should be paid to the reactions, indications and suggestions of the funding source's representatives because unwritten priorities and funding preferences which can influence the writing of the proposal will often be discovered. Modifications may also be suggested and their implications should be discussed.

At the conclusion of the meeting, the representatives of both the funding source and the institution should have the information necessary to decide whether or not the process should be pursued further. If the idea continues to interest the funding source, the meeting may end with the source requesting to make an on-site visit. If so, a date should be set and preparation for it begun.

The meeting may end with the invitation to submit a proposal. If the invitation to submit a proposal is extended and the concept paper accurately reflects the consensus of the meeting, the grantsmanship process can continue with the preparation of a proposal. If it does not accurately reflect the consensus, a modified concept paper should be prepared and submitted for review to the people within the institution concerned with the proposed idea and to the funding source's representatives to insure that there are no misunderstandings.

Regardless of the outcome of the meeting, a follow-up response is recommended. The response can be either in the form of a telephone call or a letter, thanking the representative for the time and consideration given to the proposed idea. Even if a proposal is not to be submitted, some continued linkage with the funding source may be possible that will prove beneficial at a later date.

The Contact Letter

Sometimes a grantsman will not be able to make direct contact with a funding source. Distance and cost may be prohibitive or as the *Handbook of Grants and Contracts for Non-Profit Organizations* pointed out, "Some philanthropic organizations do not permit any form of interview or personal contact."[3] If this is the case, the initial approach will be the contact letter. Care and attention must be given

---

[3]William Willner and John P. Nichols, *Handbook of Grants and Contracts for Non-Profit Organizations,* p. 168.

to drafting the letter if it is to solicit effectively the needed information and a positive response. Writing an attention-getting contact letter may be difficult. One technical assistance manual warned that, in the private sector, "Letters . . . are used so frequently by many persons that they have become an ineffective tool in solicitation."[4]

Written Contact with a Private Source—Although the contact letter is written to solicit information needed to assess the appropriateness of a funding source and to interest that source in the proposed idea, the type of letter written to private funding sources will differ somewhat from one written to public sources. The following description of a contact letter to the private sector focuses on foundations, but it is applicable to other private sources as well.

In the initial approach to the foundation, the grantsman/should address the letter to an individual rather than an office or title. From the initial research done while checking sources, the name and address of the proper contact person will usually be known. If there is some question, the letter should be addressed to the director of a program or head of the appropriate office. Receiving a letter correctly addressed is the foundation's first clue that the writer has done some investigating and has some knowledge of the organization's structure.

The contact letter should provide information for the foundation's use. The foundation will want to know the reason for writing to that particular foundation. A well written statement of reason will help underscore the sincerity of the request for information because it again gives evidence that research has been done and that the writer is not just sending out information requests to many sources. The foundation will also want to know exactly what is proposed and the credentials of the personnel and institution proposing the idea. *Eng book p.4* ✗

The contact letter should be short, generally 1-2 pages. Only concise statements of the proposed project or activity and of credentials should be incorporated in the body of the letter. The concept paper and pertinent credentials should be attached. The

---

4William A. Walker and Co., Inc., *Resource Development in the Private Sector*, p. 18.

body of the letter will also request material and/or information in those areas where the preliminary research is not adequate for assessing the appropriateness of the foundation from the institution's perspective.

In its closing, the letter will indicate the type of response or responses desired. Depending on the policy of the foundation, as well as on its geographic proximity and other factors, a more personal follow-up in the form of a telephone conference or an appointment may be possible. A personal follow-up is desirable because it gives both the foundation's representative and the institution's representative an opportunity to clear up any misunderstandings and to discuss aspects of the proposed idea that should be strengthened, emphasized or modified in some other manner.

Even though a personal follow-up is desirable, it may not be possible. In this case, the importance of the initial contact letter cannot be overemphasized. The foundation's staff will have to judge the desirability of pursuing the matter further based on the general tone and style of the letter as well as on the information it contains. Care in preparing the letter may determine whether or not the proposed idea is considered by the foundation.

Upon receipt of the letter, the individual to whom it is addressed may make a decision or may consult with other foundation members. In either case, the contact letter and the attached concept paper and credentials will be assessed from the foundation's point of view. Factors that will be weighed include:

1. What will the proposed project or activity accomplish and how important is this accomplishment to the foundation; is it a priority funding area?

2. Is the idea satisfying in terms of grant-making policy, i. e., type, length of grant period, geographic location, demographic characteristics?

3. Does the proposed project or activity overlap or duplicate another already funded or proposed; if it overlaps or duplicates one that is proposed, which appears to be a better investment of foundations funds?

4. Are the anticipated results realistic, determinable and cost effective?

5. Are the institution's and individuals' experiences and capabilities adequate?

6. Are there possible consequences that may be detrimental to the foundation?

7. Are there other possible sources of funding?

The grantsman should allow a reasonable length of time for a reply. Two to three weeks is usually a sufficient period in which to receive a reply, although the size of the foundation and its location should be considered. If a reply is not received, some kind of follow-up contact is appropriate to insure that the contact letter was received. The follow-up can be in the form of a letter inquiry, but a telephone call has the advantage of giving the caller an opportunity to clear up any foundation misgivings or misinterpretations and to ask for an appointment when feasible.

Written Contact with a Public Source—If an idea was generated in response to an announcement of a source of funds, the grantsman may already have had some written contact. For example, *The Federal Register* is the official medium for making information available to the public. In addition to announcements of new grant programs and changes in programs, it also publishes proposed guidelines and regulations. These proposed guidelines and regulations are open for a specified period of time for public comment. Individuals may send to the appropriate agency their suggestions for inclusions, modifications, and deletions, and many point out oversights, confusing terminology and procedures, etc. After the specified time, the regulations are rewritten as is deemed necessary and again published in *The Federal Register* before becoming official.

If the grantsman has been aware of a potential source of funds from the time it was announced, the research into the types of projects and activities and the method of funding will already have been done. If this is not the case, a letter should be sent to the agency or program requesting documents related to funding including the application form and instructions. Because of the requirements of the Freedom of Information Act and because of the desire to dispense their funds accountably, most agencies with grant programs have information, guidelines, application forms and other appropriate materials which they furnish on request.

Although the contact letter to a governmental source will differ from that written to a private source, it should not be an impersonal letter or one that is carelessly written. The grantsman needs the same basic information from an agency as from a foundation; and to the surprise of some inexperienced grantsmen, a governmental agency staff member may be more helpful in providing information and consultation than the staff member of a foundation.

The letter should request the desired information as well as indicate the desired response. Time and effort may also be saved if the concept paper and credentials of the institution are included in the contact letter. Most agencies are willing to go beyond mailing a packet of information. Many will provide consultation on applications, and some require a pre-application to be submitted and approved before a final application is accepted. Some federal agencies' staffs will review preliminary proposals and give their opinion on the outlook for funding. For these reasons, a personal follow-up is desirable. If a personal visit is possible, an appointment can be requested. If it is not, a telephone call may be substituted.

Assessing the Information Gathered

The responses to the contact letters and/or from meetings will indicate from the funding source's point of view whether or not the grantsmanship process should be continued. The advisability of continuing also must be assessed from the institution's point of view.

Once again, the desirability of the proposed program or activity needs to be examined. Some of the factors to be addressed include:

1. Whether a funding source's interest was sufficiently high.

2. Whether the proposed idea falls within a top priority funding area.

3. Whether the level of funding will be sufficient.

4. Whether the terms of funding are acceptable, i. e., matching funds required and the type, the funding cycle, length of grant period, chances of renewal.

5. Whether there are any restrictions or special conditions, either in eligibility procedures or funding, that make the idea less desirable.

6. Whether there are any deadlines and whether they are achievable.

If a funding source's response and the institution's assessment of the idea's continuing desirability are positive, the grantsmanship process can continue with the preparation of a proposal.

Chapter Four
GENERAL TYPES OF GOVERNMENTAL FUNDING

The Origin of Funding Authority

The "pyramid of authority" diagram is useful to help visualize where funding authority originates and how funding policies are made and changed. The authority develops downward from the top of the pyramid with each level interrelated and consistent with each other level. Change usually begins at the bottom and extends upward as high as the scope of the issue demands. If it extends to the top of the pyramid, it usually emerges as an amendment to the law.

Pyramid of Authority*

The "Sense of Congress"

Committee reports, public statements, letters, etc., of Congressmen

The Law

Regulations (Funding Criteria)

Guidelines

Appli-cation Forms & Instruc-tions | Formal Legal Opinions | Clos-ing Date Announce-ments

Policy memoranda, published articles, and public statements by governmental and agency officials

Day-to-day operating decisions, responses to specific requests, communications between national staff and the field

*Adapted from materials developed by Michael Brophy and Adrian Chan, The University of Wisconsin, Milwaukee as cited in memo from William E. Moulden, Teacher Corp, U.S.O.E. April 1, 1977

The *Law* is usually brief and is often vague and ambiguous.

The *Sense of Congress* helps to clarify the intent of the law in policy statements and it is cited in legal opinions regarding disputed points.

The *Regulations* are written to clarify the language of the law and to translate the Sense of Congress into a program that can be applied for, negotiated, operated and administered.

The *Funding Criteria* indicate how applications for funds will be evaluated. If Regulations have not been published, applications can be received and grants issued based on published funding criteria.

Guidelines are suggested models for structuring projects.

Application Forms and Instructions are consistent with the funding criteria and outline the application format.

Formal Legal Opinions are requested by national staffs concerning specific aspects and issues which apply to all funded projects.

Closing Dates and Announcements provide information on due dates for applications, the amount of money that is available for grants, the projected size of grants, and other limitations and policy features.

Policy Memoranda and Day-to-Day Operating Decisions accumulate to build up a body of "case law" which contributes to broad policy and provides answers to specific operating questions.

Contracts

The distribution of federally appropriated funds through the contract process rather than the grant process was mentioned in Chapter Three. The contract process is designed to procure or induce a desired activity whereas, in contrast, the grant process is designed to support or maintain a desired activity. The basic difference between the two processes is in the degree of control and involvement by the governmental funding source. Distributing funds via the contract process maximizes the funding source's control.

The desire on the part of many governmental sources to fund projects and activities from which the results and benefits are practical and often immediate is increasing. Senator William Proxmire's "Golden Fleece" award and well-publicized criticism of various research projects and funded activities of the federal government are indicative of the increasing emphasis on accountability. The provisions in the contract process insure that a problem will be addressed in the desired manner, otherwise the government is not obligated to pay.

It is difficult to generalize on which agencies use the grant method for distributing funds and which use the contract. In his article in the Grantsmanship Center's periodical, Keith Baker, a social science analyst in HEW, listed several agencies which are more likely to employ applied contract research: within HEW, the Offices of the Secretary and O. E.'s Office of Planning, Budgeting and Evaluation; the Departments of Labor and Housing and Urban Development; the Community Services Administration; and the National Institute of Education.[1]

The contract process begins with the decision to procure a desired activity. A team, usually headed by the project manager, prepares a Request for Proposal (RFP) which describes, in as much detail as possible, the nature of the desired activity and the anticipated methodology. When the document is ready, the RFP is distributed to institutions and organizations known to be interested and it is announced in the *Commerce Business Daily.* The announcement insures that the competition for the allotted funds is fair. The law requires that every RFP which will exceed $5,000 must be published in the *Commerce Business Daily,* but the announcement of the RFP has to be published only once. The announcement contains the address of where to write to receive a copy of the RFP.

The RFP provides a statement of the required work and some details of the anticipated methodology. It describes any available government-furnished property and provisions to be included in the contract if awarded. It may also include some guidance on how to prepare a technical portion of the proposal and/or a pricing information portion. It contains the required date for submission of proposals and the criteria that will be used to evaluate the proposals received.

In writing the proposal for a contract award, Baker offered the following advice:

1. Advance the design beyond that contained in the RPF.

---

[1]Keith Baker, "The New Contractmanship," *The Grantsmanship Center News,* March-April, 1976, p. 24.

2. Address the proposal to the audience (the review panel) and with some thought as to the possible competition.

3. Cover *all* topics listed in the criteria to be used in evaluating proposals.

4. Write clearly and creatively, but do not eliminate something from the RFP unless a strong case can be made against it.

5. Do not be overly modest; the broad areas of study design and staff capabilities will be weighed heavily and technical superiority will outweigh cost differences within reason.

6. Assemble a multi-disciplinary staff when feasible.[2]

The selection of the winning contractor is a three-step process. A technical review panel rates all the proposals submitted by the deadline and selects those that will receive further consideration. The next step is negotiation, usually face-to-face, between the potential contractor, the technical review panel and government cost experts, after which a "final and best offer" is made by the potential contractor. In the final step, the panel reviews the final offers and makes its recommendation to the contracting officer. Balancing cost against other factors, the contracting officer then selects the proposal which seems to represent the best value to the government.

The winning contractor will have some contact with two primary representatives of the funding source. The project manager, who has different titles in different agenices, is in charge of overseeing or monitoring the work to make sure that requirements are adequately met. The contractor's only independence or discretion in the project is that which is allowed by the project manager. The other representative is the contracting officer who legally has complete control over the project. This officer is the only government person who has authority to spend money and who can unilaterally, within reasonable limits, make changes in the project and override orders or promises of the project manager.

Thus, from the beginning of the process with the writing of an RFP to the end with the completion of the requirements and the payment by the contracting officer, the funding source has control.

---

[2]*Ibid.*, pp. 53-55.

Under the contract process, the authority of the project manager and the contracting officer over the contractor is virtually complete. While this fact should be considered when developing an idea in response to an RFP, Baker added that, "Due to the general reasonableness and spirit of cooperation usually found between the contractor's staff and the government's representatives, the project manager and the contracting officer rarely need to exercise their power fully."[3]

Types of Contracts

Several types of contracts are commonly used. Under the terms of a:

> *Fixed Price* contract, the contractor guarantees to deliver the contracted service or complete the contracted work within the specified period at a price agreed upon in advance and payable regardless of what the actual costs are.

> *Fixed Price with Price Revision* contract, the contractor's guarantee is the same as in a Fixed Price contract except that when the work is completed, there is a provision for negotiating the price, within preset limits, either upward or downward.

> *Cost Reimbursement* contract, the contractor is paid for allowable costs actually incurred up to a ceiling amount which is equal to the negotiated estimate of total costs stated in the contract.

> *Cost-Plus-A-Fee* contract, the contractor is paid as in a cost reimbursement contract plus a fee which may be a fixed percentage of total estimated costs or based on specified parameters such as cost, performance or schedule incentives set when the contract is negotiated.

Grants

In addition to the degree of control and involvement of the funding source, Virginia White suggested that "predictability of outcome"[4] is a determinant of which type of award instrument is

---

[3]*Ibid.*, p. 26.
[4]White, *Grants*, p. 10.

used. Grants tend to be the funding mechanism when the funds are intended to support or maintain a desired activity and where the funding source does not specify a specific end product or service. Thus, funding via the grants process encourages originality in ideas and design.

The *Federal Grant and Cooperative Agreement Act of 1977* has been passed by both the House and the Senate to establish uniform, government-wide standards for the selection of the appropriate funding mechanism. It is expected to be signed into law. The bill also calls for a detailed study of Federal assistance programs.

Under the provisions of Bill H. R. 7691, "contracts" are restricted to procurement relationships and "grants" and "cooperative agreements" are restricted to assistance relationships.

A *contract* will be used when the principal purpose is the acquisition of property or services for the direct benefit or use by the Federal government.

A *grant* will be used when the principal purpose is the transfer of money, property or services to the recipient in order to accomplish a public purpose authorized by Federal law.

A *cooperative agreement* will be used similarly to grants when substantial involvement between the Federal agency and the recipient is anticipated.[5]

Types of Grants

There are a number of different types of grants, but the ones most commonly used are:

Block (Bloc) grant is made to states or local communities for broadly defined purposes within which the recipient has flexibility in distributing the funds.

Categorical grant is similar to the Block grant except that the funds must be spent in specified categories.

Consortium grant is made to one institution in support of a project in which the program is carried out through a

---

[5] *Federal Notes* (Saratoga, California: Federal Development Associates) Vol. VIII, No. 5, October 21, 1977.

cooperative arrangement between or among the grantee institution and one or more participating institutions.

Demonstration grant is made to establish or demonstrate the feasibility of a theory or approach.

Discretionary or *Project* grant is made to fund a specific project or program with a clearly defined scope of work.

Formula grant is made when the distribution of funds is based on some formula prescribed by legislation or executive direction; the formula is generally based on such factors as population, enrollment, per capita income, or a specific need.

Planning grant is made to fund the planning, developing, designing and establishing of the means for accomplishing approved objectives.

Research grant is made to support investigation or experimentation aimed at the discovery and interpretation of facts, revision of theories based on new information, or the application of new or revised theories.

Chapter Five
WRITING THE PROPOSAL

The Information

All the efforts in developing an idea and the checking and double checking with both officials of the institution and representatives of a potential funding source have been sequential activities preceding the writing and submission of the proposal. If the grantsman has worked carefully and thoroughly through all the initial phases of the grantsmanship process, the information needed to write the proposal will be available. The concept paper which contains a summary budget, together with any modifications indicated from the responses of the potential funding source, and any guidelines and forms provided or required are the ingredients the grantsman will use in preparing the proposal.

The function of a proposal is to convince those who review it for a funding source that:

1. The idea presented is valuable because the proposed activities will solve a problem, fulfill a need, or be useful in some manner.
2. The proposed idea is within the scope of the funding source's mission and will aid in the achievement of specific goals and objectives.
3. The proposer is knowledgeable about the overall area and has the competencies and necessary facilities to carry out successfully the proposed activities.
4. The cost is justified by the anticipated results.

In its most basic terms, the proposal communicates an idea. Given that there is no substitute for a good idea, the proposal's success or failure often depends on how well it communicates the good idea. The proposal format for presenting the idea is basically the same in most instances. The method of communication should be simple, direct, clear, organized and tasteful. The "art" of grantsmanship is in communicating the idea in an organized form to a particular funding source. A good idea inadequately described or unimaginatively presented can be overlooked or misinterpreted and, consequently, can result in the proposal being rejected.

Writing the proposal is the only aspect of the entire grant process which the grantsman can control. Every applicant for funds has a grantsman's power to prepare and submit a *first class* proposal. And yet, strangely enough, it is in this phase, when the majority of the most difficult work has been completed, that the grantsmanship process breaks down. In an analysis of 700 disapproved applications to the Public Health Service, Louis E. Masterman found three major reasons for rejection. Five percent failed for a variety of reasons; of the remaining 95 percent:

1. 18% failed because of the nature of the project.
2. 38% failed because of the competency of the applicant (he noted that it was not because the applicants were incompetent but they failed to convince reviewers of their competence).
3. 39% failed because of inadequate planning and carelessly prepared applications.[1]

Proposal Format

All funding sources request basically the same information although the formality, detail and required forms can vary considerably, particularly between private and governmental sources. The following outlines the basic elements of a typical proposal and lists some of the variations in terminology:

Section I	Cover Sheet
	Application Form, Title Page
Section II	Table of Contents
Section III	Abstract
	Summary
Section IV	Problem Statement
	Needs Assessment, Questions to be
	Addressed, Project Rationale

---

[1] White, *Grants,* p. 226.

These basic elements provide an outline for writing a proposal when there are no guidelines or required forms. Even when preparing the rough draft, the major headings or sections should be established. They will not only provide keys to the reader, but also will help insure against duplication and omission and the possibility of having to make extensive revisions.

Obviously, if a funding source provides guidelines and directions, they must be followed. Occasionally, some forms, particularly of governmental agencies, will contain sections or directives that are not applicable to the proposed idea. When a section is not applicable, it *should not* be omitted. A statement explaining why the section was not addressed should be written. The penalty for not completing a section is usually to have the proposal returned or scored lower in the review process, but it can result in having the proposal rejected.

The Cover Sheet

The cover sheet is the identification tag for the proposal. It should contain all the information necessary to insure that the proposal is identified correctly and routed through the proper channels. Although the cover sheet will be the first item in the proposal, it will often be the last one completed. It will usually not be done until all the other items are assembled in final form and the proposal is ready for the authorizing signatures and submission.

The information on the cover sheet is presented in a straightforward manner and includes the following:

1. Title of the project.
2. Name of the institution submitting the proposal.
3. Name, address and telephone numbers of the project director.
4. Date of submission.
5. Name of the designated funding source.
6. Beginning and ending dates of the funding period.
7. Total funds requested, indicating first year requests if the project is multi-year.
8. Name, address, and signature of the individual(s) accepting responsibility for administration of the funds and the designated endorsement of the institution.
9. Any specialized information, i.e., the institution's IRS identification number, employer identification number, state clearinghouse number.

The title should be brief and descriptive of the proposed idea. It should avoid ambiguity and provide any casual reader with an accurate impression of what is to be accomplished. The title should be suited to the potential funding source. It should be imaginative, sometimes making possible the use of an acronym; but it should not be flippant or jargonized.

Most governmental sources provide a cover sheet and specify that it must be the first item in the proposal. Although the form varies, they ask for the same basic information.

Table of Contents

The Table of Contents is an often neglected part of the proposal. It is more than just a page reference guide. It is an outline of what is contained in the proposal and how it is organized. It should list subheadings as well as major headings and the page on which each begins. Care should be taken so that headings in the Table of Contents match those in the body of the proposal.

The Abstract

The abstract, like the cover sheet, is placed at the beginning of the proposal but is the last narrative section to be written. It is a summary of the entire proposal which contains all the key points. This condensation is a clearly and concisely written section, generally of not more than 300 words, describing:

1. The project, emphasizing timelines, significance and need.
2. The specific objectives.
3. General procedures and evaluation methods.
4. Anticipated impact of the project, emphasizing who will benefit and how.

As stated earlier, the number of proposals submitted to all funding sources has been increasing. The Research Division of the National Endowment for the Humanities reported that the number of grant applications tripled between 1970 and 1974.[2] As a result of an increasing work load, coupled with time restraints, reviewers have little time to spend attempting to understand and evaluate a particular proposal. Especially working under the government funding procedures, reviewers may have tight reading deadlines and be forced to make their evaluations of a proposal based on the careful reading of the abstract and a quicker review of the proposal. Thus, it is a good idea to include an abstract whether it is required or not.

---

[2]*Ibid*, p. 228.

The abstract should stress the needs and anticipated results of the proposed idea in a positive manner, but it should not raise controversial issues nor should it refer to the project budget or the credentials of the project staff. Considerable time and attention should be given to the writing, as well as the contents, because its quality conveys an impression of the overall quality of the proposal. For this reason, the abstract may be one of the proposal's most important sections.

The Problem Statement

The problem statement section of the proposal is the narrative section which defines and delineates the proposed idea and indicates the rationale for undertaking the proposed activities. It is usually written in two parts, the introduction, which explains the purpose and who is to be served, and the statement of needs.

The introduction functions as the lead paragraph in a news article. It establishes the background by pointing out an overall problem or need and then relating the proposed idea to it. It cites the current situation and states the nature and characteristics of the target groups or focus of the project activities. It reports on what has been done or is being done, both generally and specifically, in the same or related fields. In the introduction, the grantsman must make certain that the proposed idea is carefully defined and delineated from the larger area. It must be explained in such a way as to seem a logical part of the whole that the proposer can realistically address. Questions and problems should not be raised that the proposed activities will not address.

The statement of needs has two functions. The first is to present the rationale in such a way that the funding source agrees that there is a need for the proposed idea. In explaining the rationale, the proposal writer may cite how the project focus was identified and by whom. To present adequately the need for the proposed idea, it is often necessary to cite statistics and include other evidence such as tables, graphs, photographs, letters, and/or newspaper excerpts which substantiate the idea in a direct and sometimes dramatic way. If the supporting material is lengthy, it should be mentioned in the statement of needs with directions to refer to an indicated appendix for the complete document.

The second function of the statement of needs is to relate the proposed idea to the funding source's area of concern in such a way as to elicit its financial support. The focus of the proposed activities should be described in terms that are meaningful and relevant to the funding source and which relate directly to its priority areas. The description of the results of these activities should be realistic and logical and should carefully indicate how the anticipated outcomes will have measurable and important impact on the goals and objectives of the funding source.

Overall, the statement of the problem establishes the background, the purpose, and the significance of the proposed idea. It presents evidence that allows the funding source to make its own assessment of the need. It indicates the significance of the proposed idea to the funding source's goals and objectives in such a way that it will appear logical that the expenditure of financial resources will aid in achieving the source's mission.

The Goals

The goals are general statements of conditions that the proposer would like to have become a reality. They are value statements which bridge the gap between what the needs are and what the proposed idea is trying to do. These broad statements are usually listed in an outline with each one indicating the proposer's general direction, purpose or intention. It should be noted that the goals are not statements to be defended because they are not the target outcomes of the proposed idea. They are only indications of the proposer's desired outcomes. In writing the goals section of the proposal, the grantsman should keep in mind that a goal should be a justifiable response to an identified need. The Eckman Center in its *Grantsmanship Workplan* stated that for each goal written there should be a positive answer to the follow questions:

1. Is this one of the main reasons the project should be funded?
2. If the project were funded but at a reduced level, would this goal still be kept?
3. Would there be 100% agreement by the target group with this goal statement?
4. Is the goal statement *uniquely* related to the statement of need that was developed?

5. What aspects of the statement of needs are reflected in the goal statement?[3]

The Objectives

To justify a funding source's support, a proposed idea must have practical, attainable, and measurable results. The objectives section of the proposal relates to the goals section and consists of clear and concise statements of the anticipated outcomes within the time limits of the proposed activities. In contrast to goals, objectives state exactly what the proposed idea is expected to accomplish.

Objectives are statements concerned either with performance or management *and* with a product or process. Therefore, the objectives of the proposed idea may be of one or more of the following types:

A. Performance/Product

i.e., After a *(given)* period of time of participating in a *(specified)* activity, a *(stated)* percentage of participants will show the *(indicated)* change as evidenced by a *(particular)* measurement or evaluation technique.

B. Performance/Process

i.e., *(Given)* the establishment of a *(specified)* activity, after a *(stated)* period of time participants will be engaged in the activity an *(indicated)* percentage of the time as documented by a *(particular)* measurement device or technique.

C. Management/Product

i.e., After an *(indicated)* length of experience in a *(specified)* activity, a *(stated)* percentage or number of the product resulting from the activity will be produced in a *(given)* period of time.

D. Management/Process

i.e., By a *(given)* period of time, a *(stated)* number of

---

[3]The Eckman Center, *The Grantsmanship Workplan* (Canoga Park, California: The Eckman Center, 1975), pp. 57-58.

devices will be in operation as verified by *(specified)* evidence.

The objectives are usually presented in an itemized form and there may be more than one objective for each goal. They outline specifically what the institution intends to bring about, not the methods it will use. An objective may consist of more than one statement, but each should indicate:

1. A description of the outcome in measurable terms.
2. The criterion level for measuring the acceptability of the outcome.
3. A qualifying statement or assumption related to the conditions of measurement.

Thus, objectives are action statements indicating what is to be done, to whom it is to be done, how well it is to be done or how much is to be done, and when it is to be done.

Procedures

The procedures section provides a step-by-step description of how major aspects of the proposed idea will be carried out. It should contain enough detail to assure the funding source that the project staff knows how to go about achieving the objectives that were listed.

This section can consist of narration, charts, time schedules and any other materials that aid in describing the methodology to be used. The advice usually given for writing this section is to divide the proposed activities into phases when possible and to use a format that any competent person would be able to use as a guide in carrying out the proposed idea. The function of specialists and/or consultants, who they are and where they will be used, should be made explicit. In general, the procedures section will answer:

1. Specifically what is going to be done.
2. Specifically how it is going to be done.
3. To whom or to what it is going to be done.
4. When it is going to be done.

5. Why the particular methodology or plan of action was chosen.

A project time schedule or grid with an explanatory key is a technique often used to give an overview of the major objectives or activities in a time framework. It can be adopted for almost any type of project. The following is an example of a time grid:

XYZ Project
Project Dates from ____ to ____

OBJECTIVE AND/OR ACTIVITY	TIME PERIOD (usually in months)									
1) OBJECTIVE A	Oct	Nov	Dec	Jan	Feb	Mar	Apr	May	Ju	etc.
Activity a-1	P/I	E								
a-2	P	P	I	I	E					
2) OBJECTIVE B	P	P		I	I	I		E		
Activity b-1				P	I	E				
b-2				P/I	E					E
3) OBJECTIVE C	P	I					E			
Activity c-1					P	P	P	P	I	E
c-2		P	I	E						
4) ETC.				P	P	P	I			

KEY: P = Planning   I = Implementation   E = Evaluation

Evaluation

The evaluation section outlines a project within the proposed project. This section presents the overall evaluation process, both for assessing the on-going progress toward achieving the objectives and for assessing the actual outcome of the proposed activities. It describes the comparison procedures by which specified variables will be gauged against pre-selected standards. It establishes the boundaries of what is to be evaluated as well as indicates any independent variables, evaluation limitations and presumed causes that should be taken into consideration in interpreting and assessing the data.

The evaluation design outlines the variables to be considered, listing both general and specific considerations and the types of comparisons to be made. It is formulated in such a way that, over the time span of the proposed idea, the evaluation of those variables will perform three functions:

1. It will monitor the progress to determine whether the idea is being implemented as planned.

2. It will assess actual outcomes to determine the extent to which the objectives are being achieved.

3. It will provide the feedback necessary to assess whether modifications are necessary.

The type of data to be collected in this process is determined by the information requirements of those involved or interested in the proposed activities. Information is usually required by at least three groups who will use it in dissimilar ways. The project director and project personnel need a continuous flow of information to assess the progress of their activities. The funding source needs periodic information to keep it informed on the use of its resources and to determine the success of the activities in achieving its own goals and objectives. Project participants and/or others less directly involved need information to maintain interest in and support of the institution and its activities.

The description of the data collection methods includes the rationale for selecting a particular method and an estimate of its impact on the interpretation of the data. Although some points may not be applicable to a particular evaluation design, Norman Gold, Director, Evaluation Branch of the Office of Program Development, Office of Economic Opportunity, stated that minimally adequate coverage of the data collection phase generally includes:

61

1. Description of the specific instruments to be employed and copies of the instruments or examples of the type of content.

2. Description of how the development will proceed.
    a. History of instruments to be employed (standard tool; newly developed for this study, etc.).
    b. Reliability and validity data if available.
    c. Pretesting of new instruments

3. Description of data collection
    a. Who; relevant background characteristics.
    b. Training of data collectors.
    c. Supervision of data collectors.
    d. Reliability of data collectors.

4. Description of data collection procedures.
    a. Assignment and call back procedures
    b. Timing of data collection
        1. Beginning and ending dates
        2. Specific check or interview schedules[4]

The data analysis part of the evaluation section outlines the type of analysis to be used, the data processing steps, and the statistical techniques used. It also describes any selection and/or training of data processors. Advice often given concerning data analysis is that the statistical techniques and procedures chosen do not have to be elaborate or sophisticated, but they should be appropriate to the nature of the data collected and the information required.

Finally, the evaluation section designates those persons who will conduct the evaluation. Their experience and competency to carry out the evaluation design are also described.

Gansneder cited and explained eleven criteria useful in evaluating an evaluation design:

Internal validity refers to questions of whether the conclusions drawn will be accurate.

---

[4]Norman Gold, "Preparing an Evaluation Proposal," *Proposal Development Handbook* (University of Maryland: Center for the Study of Volunteerism, 1971), p. 69.

External validity refers to questions of whether or not the observed program effects will generalize to other populations, in other places, at other times.

Reliability refers to the question of how accurate and consistent the measures used will be.

Objectivity refers to where biases may creep into judgements made.

Relevance refers to whether the data collected will conform to the purposes of evaluation.

Importance relates to whether or not the questions raised by the evaluation will be ones that should be raised.

Scope refers to the comprehensiveness of the evaluation.

Timeliness relates to the question of whether or not the evaluation will occur at the right time and whether or not various evaluation reports will be available when they are needed.

Pervasiveness is related to the dissemination of evaluation results to all appropriate audiences.

Efficiency refers to the cost of the evaluation relative to what will be gained by doing it.[5]

The narrative portions of the proposal may also be summarized in this section. Some proposals use a Project Management Review Chart to provide a quick review of the major components of the proposed idea and their relationship to each other. Its use has several advantages:

1. It effectively displays for reviewers the detailed thought and planning that has gone into developing the proposed idea.

2. It reduces the chance that reviewers, who may be working under stringent time constraints, may overlook a significant feature of the proposed idea.

---

[5]Bruce M. Gansneder, "Program Evaluation," *Planning and Assessment in Community Education,* Harold J. Burbach and Larry E. Decker, eds. (Midland, Michigan: Pendell Publishing Co., 1977), pp. 213-214.

3. It provides project personnel with an overview of the project's complete management system and the sequential connection of the project's components.

The chart should be developed in a brief outline form with key words and the numbering system corresponding to those used in the narrative sections. The following is a sample of the form:

Project Management Review Chart

Problem or Need	Goal	Objective	Procedure or Activity	Measuring Technique	Data Analysis	Report Date

The Evaluation Design Summary is another summation technique which can have a significant positive impact on reviewers. It also provides evidence of the attention to the details that helps insure the successful implementation of the proposed idea. The Evaluation Design Summary can be adapted to many types of projects and can be used alone or in conjunction with the Project Management Review Chart. The following is a sample form:

Evaluation Design Summary

Performance Objective	Target Group	Date to Measure Record
Instrument or Technique	Data Analysis	Date to Report

Dissemination

Dissemination of information and materials is usually a part of the proposal because dissemination serves four purposes which are often important to both the proposer and the funding source:

—It informs desired groups about the project.
—It helps gain support from desired groups.
—It stimulates ideas, suggestions and constructive criticism from desired or concerned groups.
—It makes available information which may be of value to others with similar problems or needs.

This section of the proposal details the planning of the dissemination efforts including the subjects or materials to be disseminated, the audience, the methods and the time schedule.

It describes how the outcomes of the proposed idea together with the conclusions and recommendations are to be reported. In this section, the proposal writer must be practical and realistic in anticipating the likely outcomes and their significance and/or effect on others. Possible benefits should be listed indicating to whom and how. If the proposed idea apparently will develop innovative techniques and approaches or will develop materials, plans, etc. of interest to others, the procedures for making these outcomes available should be outlined. How their availability will be made known, together with how they will be produced and distributed or made accessible should also be explained. Any possible transferability of the proposed idea to other areas should be indicated, as well as any future projections.

The dissemination section is usually the final narrative section dealing specifically with the proposed idea. It should be imaginative and forward-looking but it should also be realistic and practical because it is the last opportunity to testify to the value of the proposed idea. In general, this section should emphasize any reasonably anticipated outcomes or activities that are desirable or useful, and any plans or procedures for making them available to others.

Facilities

The facilities section provides information concerning the

environment and materials needed to carry out the proposed idea. Detailing what is available assures the funding source that meticulous and thorough attention has been given to anticipating needs. Any specialized feature or superiority of facilities or equipment should be emphasized.

If cooperative arrangements have been made for the use of personnel, facilities, equipment, etc., the terms of the agreement should be indicated. A copy of the agreement or authorization should be included, usually in the appendices.

Personnel

The personnel section identifies the principal people involved in the proposed idea. It consists of naming them and emphasizing their special areas of expertise. Their overall qualifications and background are usually indicated by the inclusion of their vitae in the appendices.

Cooperative arrangements involving personnel outside the institution should be explained and vitae or other documentation of their competency included. Specialists, consultants, etc. who will be involved should also be identified and their qualifications documented.

This section should also contain a brief description of the institution. It is important to demonstrate the basic compatibility between the institution and the proposed idea. Specific areas supporting this compatibility should be emphasized with the history and other documentation included in the appendices.

Budget

The budget is a working document which forms a basis for action for both the potential funding sources and the institution. The amount of detail it contains is dependent upon the nature of the proposed idea, what is needed to explain reasonably the financial requirements of the proposed activities, and the breakdown of costs requested by the potential funding source.

The budget has two functions. The first function is to record as realistically as possible the cost of achieving the objectives stated in the proposal. The itemized figures should contain no surprises and should accurately reflect what was stated in the various narrative sections. The potential funding source will use the figures to determine whether the proposed idea is economically realistic and feasible. The budget's second function is to provide the institution with a means to monitor the financial activities over the funding period. Used in this way, the budget figures provide comparisons to determine if the progress toward achieving the objectives is being made within the established financial limits.

The budget summarizes a great deal of information concerning the proposed idea. It reflects costs which are fairly easy to determine as well as costs that are difficult to estimate either because they are indirectly related to the proposed activities or because they may fluctuate depending on varying circumstances. To fulfill the budget's functions effectively, however, the figures must be as realistic and as accurate as possible.

Both the case of overstating costs and the case of understating costs create problems. Costs are usually underestimated for one of several reasons:

1. A major cost is overlooked or forgotten and not included.

2. Miscellaneous and sundry details of carrying out the proposed idea are overlooked and their costs are consequently not included.

3. The estimates are made too conservatively because the motivation is to keep costs down to increase the likelihood of funding.

Whatever the reason, underestimating can not only put severe financial strain on the successfully funded proposal but also can cause the proposer to appear incompetent to a funding source. Overstating the costs, either because of overestimating expenses or because of padding expenses to insure against underestimating them, can also create a negative impression because most funding sources have fairly accurate information on different types of expenses.

A recommended technique to help insure that costs have been estimated realistically vis-a-vis the project objectives and proposed activities is to give advance thought to three possible budgeting conditions. In the first situation, costs are estimated in terms of the level of expenses that would be incurred if the project were carried out in the manner proposed in the procedures section of the proposal. This "ideal" budget reflects the costs that would be incurred if the proposer were given the level of funding it believes necessary to finance the scope of the idea as it envisions it. The use of the term "ideal" does not mean that the budget is padded. Because a funding source has an accurate idea of the costs of certain kinds of activities, padding expenses risks receiving a negative reaction to the proposal.

A second type of budgeting condition arises when a funding source is interested in the proposed idea but it is not willing to fund it at the level proposed in the "ideal" budget. This condition also occurs when some costs in the "ideal" budget are deemed unallowable. In either case, costs are pared to a level estimated to be sufficient to carry out project activities even though the scope or impact of the proposed idea is somewhat reduced. The "adequate" budget reflects where the proposer believes expenses can be cut without sacrificing the achievement of the project's objectives.

The third budgeting condition arises when costs must be reduced below the level estimate in the "adequate" budget. In this case, in which the project will be significantly altered, the objectives are prioritized and advance thought is given to objectives or activities which can be cut from the project to reduce costs to a level that the source is willing to fund. The "compromise" budget details the costs that would be incurred if these cuts were made. It reflects the resulting altered project which is still of value to both the proposer and the funding source. Giving advanced thought to this compromise condition will be beneficial in the event that budget negotiations are necessary.

In order for the figures to be as accurate as possible, the budget preparation will usually be a joint effort. Whether it is prepared by a budget committee or by a designated person, it is a good idea to have individuals within the institution who have budgetary experience or specialized knowledge review the figures. One person who should be included in the preparation process when possible is the institutional officer who must approve the budget and who will sign the financial reports. Virginia White cautioned:

> Expertise in budget preparation, as in other things, is learned by experience but also as in other things. . . experience is not always transferable—costs vary in different localities, institutional policies vary

remarkably. The experienced applicant dealing with a new institution may need as much guidance as the totally inexperienced one.[6]

The total budget for the proposed idea is the sum of the direct and indirect costs associated with effecting the proposed activities. It outlines the major categories of expenses for each type of cost. In addition, it can also show the institution's commitment to the idea. Even if a potential funding source does not require the institution's financial support, it is a good idea to point out its contribution when possible. Its contributions can be cash or in-kind.

The terms most often used to describe institutional contributions are "cost-sharing arrangements" and "matching funds." Matching funds are cash outlays by the institution according to the ratio established by the potential funding source. Cost sharing usually implies donated services and materials, often called "in-kind" contributions. These in-kind contributions are personnel, services and facilities available for use in implementing the proposed idea, which are given a dollar equivalent value and included in the budget to indicate institutional support.

Direct Costs—If a budget form is not provided, the costs directly associated with project activities are usually broken down into the following categories:

1. Personnel. This category includes the wages and salaries of professional and clerical persons employed full- or part-time in the project. Also included are fringe benefit costs and, if the fiscal period extends beyond one year, merit and inflation based raises.

2. Outside Services. These costs are consultant and service contracts. Consultant costs are usually short-term and include both travel and fee.

3. Supplies. In addition to consumable supplies used on the project, this category includes instructional and training supplies, such as books, video tapes, etc.

4. Equipment. The category includes purchase and rental costs as well as amounts allotted to maintenance and repair.

[6]White, *Grants*, p. 244.

5. Travel and Transportation. All travel and related subsistence costs directly incurred are included.

6. Communications. This category includes telephone installation and service; toll calls; messenger, cable, and telegraph service; postage, etc.

7. Publications. The costs are given for printing, publishing, and/or duplication of brochures, reports, reprints, as well as any dissemination costs not included elsewhere.

8. Other Costs. This category covers miscellaneous items not included elsewhere, such as cost of computer time and necessary supporting services, facility rental, minor alterations, fees to participants.

Indirect Costs—Indirect costs are the overhead charged to the proposed activities. They are the costs incurred in the general support and management of the proposed activities and are often called the project overhead. Examples of these costs are:

1. General administration and general expenses such as accounting, payroll, administrative offices.

2. Research administration.

3. Departmental administration expense.

4. Plant operation and maintenance, such as utilities, janitorial services, routine maintenance and repairs.

5. Depreciations and use allowance.

Indirect costs are usually calculated as a percentage of a base figure. Generally they are an agreed upon percentage of:

1. salary and wages, often excluding fringe benefits, or
2. total direct costs.

Educational and other tax-exempt, non-profit institutions receiving federal support often have a predetermined rate, called a negotiated fixed indirect cost rate that is acceptable to most federal granting sources. The rate is usually expressed as a percentage of salaries and wages or of total direct costs. When this rate is not acceptable, the program guidelines should indicate the allowable rate. It should be noted that some federal programs and private foundations do not allow the inclusion of indirect costs in the budget, but the program guidelines will indicate when indirect costs are not allowable.[7]

The indirect cost percentage allowed by foundations is usually established as a part of their granting policy or is negotiated individually for each grant. In the latter case, agreement is reached prior to funding the proposal.

Budget Worksheet

As stated earlier, the budget details the costs which will be incurred in successfully effecting the proposed idea. Thus, the categories used should not hide costs or present a vague explanation of the reason for incurring a cost. If an item is mentioned in the narrative portion of the proposal, it should appear as a budget item. The reverse should also be true, if an item appears in the budget it should be found in the narrative.

Some funding sources have budget forms but often the form is brief and expenses are grouped into major categories. Federal agencies, in particular, use this type of budget form which usually has the following categories:

A. Personnel
B. Fringe Benefits
C. Travel
D. Equipment
E. Contractual
F. Construction
G. Other
H. Total Direct Charges
I. Total Indirect Charges
J. Totals

In preparing the budget a more detailed breakdown may be useful. The budget worksheet presents all the items in a major category and indicates how the individual items were estimated. The completed worksheet is often included in the proposal as an addendum, even when there is another required budget form, because of its explanatory features. The following is a sample of a budget worksheet:

---

[7]*Ibid*, p. 188 ·

Budget for 12 Months

OTHER BUDGET INFORMATION Object Cost Description	Grant Funds Required 1	Matching Funds by Institution 2	Others Matching Source 3	Total 4
A) Personnel (S&W)	6,000			
a-1 Project Director based upon .50 FTE for 12 months— Salary $24,000	6,000	6,000		12,000
a-2 Associate Project Director Based upon 1. FTE for 12 months—Salary $18,000	12,000	6,000		18,000
a-3 Four IHE project training staff projected for 29 days; average total salary $100.00 per day.		2,000	900	2,900
a-4 Graduate Student Assistants based on 15 hours per week @ $4.00 per hour x 40 weeks	2,400			2,400
a-5 Sec./Clerical 1. FTE Based on State Civil Service Class C	7,000			7,000
Sub-Totals for Personnel	27,400	14.000	900	42,300
B) Fringe Benefits				
b-1 F.B. for project staff (a-1) (a-2) (a-3) Based upon 15% of S&W Includes FICA, Soc. Sec., Life and Medical Ins. and Retirement	2,700	2,100	135	4,935
b-2 Sec/Clerical F.B. based (a-5) on 12% of S&W	840			840
b-3 Graduate Student F. B. based on 7% of S&W (a-4)	168			168
Sub-Totals for Fringe Benefits	3,708	2,100	135	5,943
C) Travel				
c-1 Project Staff—based on three trips to Wash., D. C., @ $120 and 16 field trips @ average of $45 per trip for transportation and diem	1,080			1,080

	Grant Funds Required 1	Matching Funds by Institution 2	Others Matching Source 3	Total 4
c-2 Travel 20 Field Associates to four inservice meetings @ $40 per trip x 4 x 20	3,200			3,200
c-3 National 3 day training workshops for Project Staff to be held Aug. in Atlanta, Ga., 6 @ $175.00	1,050			1,050
D) Equipment				
d-1 one ABC Typewriter Model A-1 @ $564.00	564			564
d-2 one tape recorder Model AMEN @ $159	159			159
E) Supplies				
e-1 General Office @ $50 per month x 12 months	400	200		600
e-2 Instructional supplies for 20 field Assoc. 4 meetings @ $5 per meeting 20 x 20	400			400
e-3 Xeroxing and Printing 250 copies of 4 booklets @ $1.00 per copy = 1,000 and Xerox @ $30 per month x 12	1,360			1,360
e-4 Postage & Communication Based on 2050 first class @ $0.24 ave. and monthly freight @ $60/mo. x 12 months	1,215			1,215
F) Construction none required				
G) Other				
g-1 Room rental charge Conference Centers for Inservice training	700		600	1,300
g-2 Consultant for process facilitator and training 3 days @ $100 plus expenses @ $50 per day	450			450

	Grant Funds Required 1	Matching Funds by Institution 2	Others Matching Source 3	Total 4
g-3 Consultant for External Evaluation 6 days @ $100 plus 6 days expenses @ $50/day	900			900
g-4 Long Distance phone based on 20 calls per month @ $3.40 x 12 all local and in-state local funds $50 per month x 12	816	600		1,416
H) Total Direct Charges	43,402	16,900	1,635	61,937
I) Total Indirect Charges Requested based upon 8% allowable cost of grant for DTC Note: negotiated approval rate with US Government based upon A-91 CBC = 33%	3,472	1,352	131	4,955
J) Totals	46,874	18,252	1,766	66,892
% for funding Contributions	70%	27%	3%	
K) Program Income none				

*Note: 30% Matching funds required from institutional and all other funding sources in this sample budget.

Budget Justifications

The budget justification is in effect an appendix of the budget and is used to explain budget line items. It may also be used to explain any item in the budget which might seem unusual or might raise questions concerning the proposed activities. Unusual costs in any budget category, such as purchase of an unusual volume of books or materials, or large subcontracting costs, should be noted and explained in the budget justification. If the various sections of the proposal have been well written, budget line items should not contain any surprises. The inclusion of the annotated notes at the end of the budget, however, makes the reason for the item immediately identifiable and is often an aid to a reviewer.

Appendices

The appendices of the proposal contain the supportive material and documents which are not included in the main body of the proposal. Each section of the proposal should be as brief and concise as possible. When relevant supportive material exists, the section should contain a brief statement about it and the reason for its inclusion. Directions should then be given to refer to the indicated appendix for the complete document.

The appendices will usually include:

1. The history and relevant background of the institution.
2. Credentials of the personnel involved.
3. Relevant studies and/or research projects.
4. Relevant charts, graphs, or other explanatory material.
5. Copies of evaluation instruments and/or examples of types of content.
6. Copies or samples of materials developed for the proposed project.
7. Copies of letters supporting the need for the proposed project and/or the institution's capability to implement it successfully.

Letters of Support

Even though the inclusion of support letters was mentioned in the section on appendices, their potential impact deserves an additional note. The support letters provide the potential funding source with documented evidence of others' evaluation of the need for the proposed idea, the feasibility of the plan of action and the institution's capabilities for achieving the proposed goals and objectives. Typically, the letters are written by an official or a representative of an institution, agency, organization and/or group interested or involved in the project.

Because of their potential influence on a potential funding source's decision, the support letters should be prominently placed in the appendices. Sometimes, because of its nature or importance, a particular letter will also be used or referred to in the body of the proposal, usually in the introduction.

Chapter Six
SUBMISSION AND FOLLOW UP

Submission to the Institution

Official Signature—When the writing has been completed, the document typed on the proper forms or in an organized format and proofed and the budget figures and calculations double checked, the proposal should be submitted to the appropriate institutional officer for signature. Both the institution and the funding source require the signature of the authorized representative of the institution certifying that the institution will honor any commitments made in the proposal. If the grantsmanship process has been followed, obtaining the signature should be a minor procedure. It is sometimes helpful if the official signature is obtained before the required number of copies of the proposal is made so that each copy will have the signature without the official having to sign multiple copies.

Letter of Transmittal—Even if a letter of support is already included, one other type of letter is usually enclosed with the proposal, but is not attached to it. The letter of transmittal is a brief letter usually signed by the official whose signature appears on the cover sheet requesting that the potential funding source consider the enclosed proposal.

Date of Submission

If there is a deadline by which the potential funding source must receive the proposal if it is to be considered, this date should figure prominently in the timing allowed for writing the proposal and obtaining the required signatures. Endorsement procedures vary widely among institutions. Some institutions require a formal review by a Policy Board before the authorized signature is affixed. In others, obtaining the signature may be as simple as walking into the appropriate office and requesting it. But whatever the procedure, the grantsman should be sure that the deadline will not be exceeded. The postmarked or certified mailing date on the proposal which precedes the closing date can mean the difference between competing for funds or not competing.

Transmittal of the Proposal

The proposal package submitted to the potential funding source consists of three parts: the cover sheet, the letter of transmittal, and the proposal with its appendices. The cover sheet and proposal pages should be assembled in a manner that will hold them securely. The method of transmittal will depend on time requirements. If time permits, the proposal package may be mailed or shipped via messenger service or other transmittal alternatives. If the deadline is near, the proposal may be hand delivered. Whatever the case, care should be taken to insure that the package reaches its designated destination in time to be considered.

Post-Application Phase

The post-application phase is a difficult time for many grantsmen. It is the waiting period when the initiative is up to the potential funding source. Many feel an urge to do something, but most agree that there is little that can be done and caution against any interference in the review and award process.

Some actions may be possible under certain circumstances. If there is no date set by which the notification of award will be made, and if there has been no acknowledgement of the receipt of the proposal, it is acceptable to inquire about its receipt. Another possible reason for contacting the potential funding source is if new material or information arises that is significant to the proposal. But the advice generally given, although difficult to follow, is to wait patiently.

Proposal Review

The review process followed will depend on the funding source to whom the proposal was sent; but regardless of the process used, the purposes of the review are basically the same. Governmental review procedures are specific and a funding source will describe them to any applicant if asked. Proposals usually undergo a review by staff members of the funding source and by a selected review panel. An effort is made to insure that each proposal meeting submission requirements will receive unbiased consideration. Private funding sources are not bound by the Freedom of Information Act. Their review procedures are generally not as specific and they may be unwilling to provide information regarding the review process.

In the review process of most sources, the proposal usually will be read by reviewers who then make recommendations to those empowered to award the grants. The reviewers are asked to consider whether:

1. The proposal does (does not) meet application requirements.

2. The proposal is (is not) within the funding source's priorities or area of responsibility; many times this selection process is a staff function completed before an outside review panel starts its review process.

3. The proposed idea is (is not) needed in the indicated area.

4. The proposed idea is (is not) of value to the funding source.

5. The proposer does (does not) indicate an understanding of the problem and an awareness of the state of the art concerning that problem.

6. The proposer does (does not) indicate a soundness of approach.

7. The proposer has (has not) the necessary capabilities and experiences.

8. The proposal is realistic (unrealistic) in terms of the level of cost and effort vis-a-vis the proposed objectives.

9. The proposed budget is realistic (unrealistic).

10. Other sources of funding are (are not) possible.

11. Negative consequences are (are not) likely to occur.

12. Other proposals are (are not) superior.

Outcomes of Proposal Review
Several outcomes are possible from the review process:

1. Request for additional information.
The grantsman should provide only what is requested, as quickly as possible.

2. A request to modify the proposal, usually in terms of limiting project activities or decreasing the amount of funds requested.

The grantsman in consultation with other members of the institution must assess the effect of the modification on the proposed idea. If it seems that modifications are possible without jeopardizing the achievement of objectives or the quality of the proposed activities, a conference should be arranged between representatives of the institution and the funding source to work out specific details. If compromises can be agreed upon, the proposal then can be revised accordingly.

3. Request for an oral presentation.

Requesting an oral presentation is becoming more frequent, especially on the part of governmental sources. The receipt of such a request usually means that the review process has narrowed the selection to two or three proposals. The individual making the presentation should remember that the funding source already likes the proposal or the request would not have been made. Consequently, the presentation is not a defense of the proposal.

If the funding source does not provide any information on the aspects of the proposal in which it is especially interested, an effort should be made to determine the identity of the individuals who will attend the presentation as well as their areas of interest. The presentation can then emphasize these areas. If no information or guidelines are available regarding which aspects of the proposal to emphasize, the presentation should be geared toward pointing out those aspects which the institution believes to be especially significant. But whatever the emphasis, the individual making the presentation should be thoroughly familiar with the proposal and the presentation should be consistent with what is contained in the proposal.

4. Request for a site visit.

Site visits are required by statute for certain types of projects funded by governmental sources. But site visits may be desirable even when they are not required, especially if the proposal requests a sizeable grant or long-range support. At the time arrangements are made, the format of the visit will be specified. It is then usually the responsibility of the project director to see that the requests are met.

Site visits usually are made to see specific facilities and to talk to the project director and others involved in the proposed activities. They also provide another method of assessing the institution's support. Site visits are generally short and restraint is advisable. In the case of federal projects, not only is "wining and dining" visitors unnecessary, it is illegal.

5. Notification of the proposal's rejection.

The first action taken should be to write a letter to the funding source, indicating that the proposer does not desire to sever relations with the funding source because of the rejection of its proposal. The positive tone of the letter will help to maintain communication ties that may be valuable in the future.

An inquiry should be made into the reasons for the decision. Under the Freedom of Information Act, governmental sources are required to explain their decision. Many agencies making grants have specific procedures to be followed when an institution wants to know why its proposal was rejected. For example, in the case of HEW, a debriefing session may even be requested. A breakdown of evaluation criteria may be requested and questions may be asked about the proposal's deficiencies. Also, under the requirements of the Freedom of Information Act, an unsuccessful applicant can ask for a copy of the winning proposal, except when it contains patentable information.

If the reasons for the proposal's rejection can be determined, it may be possible to revise the proposal and resubmit it to another source. Even if resubmission is not possible, knowledge about the reasons for rejection can be helpful in writing a future proposal possibly to be submitted to that particular funding source.

6. Official notification of the receipt of a grant.

A letter of official acceptance signed by the project director or the official responsible for the administration of the funds may be required, especially if the funds are received from a governmental source. If official acceptance is not required, the immediate response is a thank you letter.

The initial response begins the follow-through communication with the funding source. The names of the appropriate staff members should be placed on the project's mailing list to insure that all pertinent materials are sent to them. They also should be invited to visit the project and to attend relevant meetings, workshops and conferences when possible. Every effort should be made to keep the representatives of the funding source fully informed as the grant is implemented.

The technical assistance manual for *Resource Development in the Private Sector* contains the following reminder of the importance of these kinds of follow-through activities:

> The ultimate goal of a successful fund-raising program is to develop a constituency who will continue to support the program. The follow-through which continues after the initial grant has been awarded, can assist in encouraging a donor to become personally involved in the project and to become a continual supporter.[1]

---

[1]William A. Walker and Company, Inc., *Resource Development in the Private Sector*, p. 26.

Chapter Seven
GRANT ADMINISTRATION

A Part of the Process

Grant administration refers to the activities that occur after funding notification has been received. Many grantsmanship books, articles and discussions conclude with little or no mention of this area. But grant administration is as much a part of the grantsmanship process as idea generation, research of funding sources and proposal development.

One reason for the scant treatment of grant administration is the wide variation in requirements among funding sources. Although Patricia Jenkins was referring to federal sources, the following comment is applicable to other sources as well:

> One of the most confusing parts of the federal grant process for many nonprofit organizations is what to do after a grant has been received: What financial and programmatic records must be kept? What reports must be made? When will grant payments be received? How can changes be made in a project budget? What happens to unspent funds?[1]

After pointing out that there are many questions, all of which need answering, she added the additional observation that "to make things still more complicated different federal agencies often have different answers."[2]

Although the grant administration area is confusing and often complicated, a grantee cannot afford to ignore it or treat it lightly. A grant is a legal agreement. The questions must be answered because, as Jenkins also pointed out, "the potential consequences of not finding the right answers can be severe."[3]

---

[1]Patricia Jenkins, "Guide to the New Grants Administration Standards for Non Profits," *The Grantsmanship Center News*, Nov.-Dec. 1976, p. 33.

[2]*Ibid.*

[3]*Ibid.*

The first step in the grant administration process is to answer the questions concerning procedures and requirements. Most often, many of the answers can be found in the funding source's formal notice of the award of a grant.

Notice of Grant Award

The notice of grant award usually does three things:

1. It gives formal notice to the grantee and others of the awarding of funds.

2. It refers to the terms and conditions under which the funds are granted.

3. It provides the documentary evidence for recording the funds in the accounting system with assigned project numbers.

The form of the formal notification will vary with different sources as will the procedures and requirements it details. In almost all cases, however, a careful reading of the notice will answer questions about the terms and conditions under which the grant is made.

Although the form and content of the notice of grant award are far from standardized, the specifications for an HEW notice provide a good indication of the type of information it contains. The staff manual states:

A notice of grant award shall:

A. State legal name of grantee and the name of the granting agency.

B. 1. State amount being awarded.

2. If grant is awarded under the project period system, also state:

a. Amount authorized for budget period for which current grant is made and dates of that budget period.

b. Cumulative total of Federal funds authorized to date and the amount recommended for each subsequent budget period.

3. If not under project period, state dates of grant period if applicable.

C. State purpose of the grant.

D. Incorporate by reference the application for the grant including amendments.

E. Cite the legislative authority and regulations under which the grant is made.

F. Incorporate by reference any Grants Administration Manual chapters or policy statements which are not incorporated into the application regulations and which are intended to be made legally binding on the grantee.

G. Include or incorporate by reference all terms, conditions or grant clauses that are required by the Department, granting agency or program policies to be incorporated into each individual grant award.

H. Include any special conditions for the grant prescribed on or with the list of approved or disapproved grant applications.

I. Include any other special terms or conditions . . .

J. If not clearly stated in preceding, state:

1. Performance and financial reporting requirements applicable to the grant including the frequency and contents of reports.

2. Prior approval requirements applicable to the grant and how approval may be obtained.

K. Name any key personnel, i. e., principal investigator or project director whose qualifications were the reason for the approval of the grant.

L. Identify the Department official or officials responsible for the administration of the grant.

M. Set forth on its face information needed for the fiscal administration of the grant, the address of the grantee and the address of its business office and the accounting classification numbers.

N. State name and address of the Federal payment office and

the title and telephone number of the HEW official to be contacted in regard to payments.

O. Be signed by the signature of:

    1. Head of the agency, or

    2. Grants officer[4]

Financial Procedures

After determining the terms and conditions under which funds are awarded, the next step in grant administration is to make provisions in the institution's budget and finance office and in the accounting system. The accounting principles for nonprofit institutions differ from those of commercial institutions because their exemption from taxes imposes restrictions on the use of funds. The financial records of nonprofit institutions must be able to show that exemption requirements were met. Until recently, this area of grant administration has created some problems for some institutions. There have been questions regarding what constitutes "generally accepted" accounting principles for nonprofit institutions.

The American Institute of Certified Public Accountants (AICPA) has been addressing this problem area. It is in the process of publishing "audit guides" containing standards of generally accepted accounting principles for nonprofit institutions. Three audit guides are currently in use:

a. *Audits of Voluntary Health and Welfare Organizations,* issued in 1974 ($4.50).

b. *Audits of Colleges and Universities,* issued in 1973 ($5).

c. *Hospital Audit Guide,* issued in 1972 ($4).

A fourth guide is now in draft form. A copy of this proposed guide, entitled *A Tentative Set of Accounting Principles and Reporting Practices for Nonprofit Organizations Not Covered by Existing AICPA Industry Audit Guides,* is available free of charge from AICPA.

The basic reference of accounting practices for federally funded

---

4*Grants Administration Manual,* Department Staff Manual, HEW, 1976, Section 1-67-20.

projects is the Office of Management and Budget Circular A-110, entitled *Uniform Administrative Requirements for Grants and Agreements with Institutions of Higher Learning, Hospitals and other Nonprofit Organizations*. A copy is available free of charge from the Publication Office, Office of Management and Budget, 726 Jackson Place, N.W., Washington, D. C. 20503.

Although the accounting systems of various institutions will differ, each system should serve several common functions.

Internally, the accounting system should provide:

—Fiscal data on which to base budgets and other planning decisions.

—An accurate record of incoming money and in-kind contributions.

—Continuous recording and control of expenditures.

—Periodic comparisons of actual income and expenditures with budgeted expectations, broken down into budget categories.

—Cost information for program evaluation.[5]

Externally, the accounting system should meet the requirements of regulatory and governmental bodies, funding sources and others concerned with the responsible dispensation and/or use of funds.

Willner and Hendrick listed three provisions which must be made in an institution's accounting system when a grant is received:

1. Control of internal numbering system.

2. Establishment of budget within the institution's accounting system.

3. Control of line items.[6]

The first provision means that account numbers are issued to identify the funds. This identification number is especially important

[5]Patricia Jenkins, "Guide to Accounting for Nonprofits," *The Grantsmanship Center News,* April-June, 1977, p. 10.

[6]William Willner and Perry B. Hendricks, Jr., *Grants Administration* (Washington, D.C.: National Graduate University, 1972), p. 111.

if the institution receives more than one grant or funds from more than one source.

The second provision is the breakdown of the proposal budget, as approved, into categories and accounts which fit the institution's accounting system. Assigning account numbers to the various budget categories allows transactions to be grouped together in a systematic manner. It also simplifies the work to be done in preparing financial statements and reports because a breakdown of data is readily available.

The final provision is part of the internal control system which is composed of procedures and cross checking designed to minimize the likelihood of misappropriation of assets or misstatement of accounts and to maximize the likelihood of detection if either situation occurs. This provision means that restrictions on shifting of funds from one category to another are taken into consideration and that the shifting of funds is systematized to insure that requirements are met and that funds can be traced.

Careful attention to financial procedures is an important part of grant administration. Complete and accurate records are essential to provide the financial information needed for decision making, for effective planning, and for efficient operation of the institution in general. The financial records are also of importance to others outside the institution. Their concern for the completeness and accuracy of these records is underscored by the fact that many funding sources require an audit of financial records.

Auditing

Auditing, as defined by Gross, is:

A series of procedures followed by an experienced professional accountant used to test, on a selective basis, transactions and internal controls in effect, all with a view to forming an opinion of the fairness of the presentation of the financial statements for the period. An audit is not an examination of every transaction that has been recorded; it is a series of tests designed to give the accountant a basis for judging how effectively the records were kept and the degree of reliance he can place on the internal controls.[7]

---

[7]Malvern Gross, Jr., *Financial and Accounting Guide for Nonprofit Organizations* (New York: Ronald Press, 2nd Ed., 1974).

An audit is often required by a funding source to assess the credibility of the grantee's financial reports and to insure that the financial requirements of the grant agreement have been met. An indication of the types of deficiencies in financial records which an audit can disclose is provided by the results of an audit of 11 agencies receiving grants from the National Institute of Drug Abuse. Deficiencies were found in 10 of the 11 projects' accounting systems and/or financial records. The deficiencies included:

—The lack of a procurement system.

—No written policy for reimbursement of employee business travel expenses.

—No comparison of expenditures to budget.

—No financial statements.

—The use of funds budgeted for the following month to pay current monthly expenses.

—No systematic recording of project revenues and costs in appropriate books of records.

—No control records for physical assets.

—Delays or failure to post and close accounts.[8]

Other Grant Administration Considerations

Other steps in grant administration are difficult to detail because they vary widely depending on the funding source, type of grant and the nature of the project. The circular mentioned in the Financial Procedures section published by the Office of Management and Budget (OMB Circular A-110) also contains a set of regulations intended to standardize the management policies which federal agencies use for grants to nonprofit institutions. The categories covered in the OMB Circular A-110 provide an indication of other areas which need to be considered in administering a grant. The categories are:

grant payment
matching share

---

[8] An article in the *Chronicle of Higher Education,* February 28, 1977.

cash depositories
financial management systems
procurement standards
property management
bonding and insurance
program income
reporting requirements
program performance
budget provision
grant closeout procedures
suspension and termination
records retention

Edward Grove, who as deputy controller of Ingham County, Maryland oversees the administration of federal funds, stated that it is questionable whether the regulations in OMB Circular A-110 and its counterpart for state and local governments FMC 74-7 will become policy for all agencies. But he pointed out that "as a guide to introduce people to grantsmanship, [the Circular] is the greatest tool in the world because it gives them some kind of a guideline, something as a norm to work from."[9]

The Grant Administrator

The person performing the grant supervision duties is usually called the grant administrator. It is the grant administrator's role to minimize any frictions and constraints that may occur between the grantee and grantor while at the same time insuring that the terms of the grant are fulfilled. A study which, among other things, was conducted on the major roles or types of action of a grant administrator in an institution of higher education identified five.

1. Internal Administrator which included a broad spectrum of skills related to the day-to-day management of office staff, the record system, relationships with other administrators in the home institution and communicating about grant proposals.

---

[9] Jenkins, "Guide to New Grants Administration Standards for Non Profits," p. 35.

2. Group Expeditor which included expediting grant proposals and information; coordinating the activities of many specialists; and possessing a broad range of knowledge, the ability to listen and comprehend, and the ability to mobilize decision making for group problems.

3. Business Manager which included efficiently using time, being fiscally meticulous, being sensitive to budget matters, possessing a high tolerance for paper work, and serving as a spokesman for sound administrative procedures.

4. Educational Specialist which included demonstrating general interest in the total education process of home institution to others, possessing strong writing and speech skills, and indicating the ability to stand firm on decisions once they are made.

5. External Coordinator which included acting as intermediary between home institution and outside agencies, being heavily involved in activities with federal agencies, providing information to faculty from these contacts, having the ability to display humility in relationships with faculty and having the ability to foresee future developments and their potential.[10]

In general, the grant administrator's role includes being both a manager and a middleman. As a manager, the grant administrator coordinates the activities discussed in the preceding section as well as the supportive services needed to carry out the proposed activities and to fulfill the terms of the grant agreement. As a middleman, the administrator interprets the institution's position in the grant's contract to project personnel and, in turn, their position to the institution. Willner and Hendricks referred to the grant administrator as a coordinator but pointed out that the ". . .authority may vary but it must include control of terms and conditions of the grant and the budget and the authority to make the project work without undue red tape or restrictions."[11]

---

[10]James J. Pallante, Gerald W. McLaughlin and John C. Smart, "A Role Analysis of Higher Education Grant Administrators," *Journal of the Society of Research Administration,* Newport Beach, Calif., Vol. VI, No. 2, Fall, 1974, pp. 22-23.

[11]Willner and Hendricks, *Grants Administration,* p. 123.

The Project Director

Although the grant administrator coordinates and manages the supportive services, effecting the actual activities of the funded project is the responsibility of the project director. This person, often called the principal investigator, implements the plan of action outlined in the funded proposal. It is the project director's responsibility to manage and coordinate project activities and personnel to insure that time lines are followed, goals and objectives are achieved and programmatic reporting requirements are fulfilled.

An Additional Note

Although the grant administrator and the project director are both concerned with the same funded proposal, the focus of each one's responsibilities are different. The grant administrator's responsibilities are focused more on the legal aspects of grant administration and on supplying services designed to aid the project activities and project personnel. The project director's responsibilities focus more on insuring that project activities and personnel achieve the proposed goals and objectives. Thus, while occasionally the duties of grant administrator and the project director may be handled by one person, generally they will not be.

For example in institutions of higher education, the grant administrator is usually a person in the Office of Sponsored Programs or in the Accounting Office. The project director is usually a faculty member or a person hired to supervise the project activities. In other institutions, the grant administrator frequently will be a person in the accounting section of the home office while the project director may be a staff person or a person on-site.

The likelihood that the grant administration responsibilities will be divided between the grant administrator and the project director as presented in this chapter increases with:

a. The size of the institution seeking grant funds.

b. The frequency with which grant funds are sought.

c. The sophistication or complexity of the proposed project.

Chapter Eight
CONCLUSION

Funding Process

Grantsmanship has been defined as a process which involves sequential activities. Distinct phases can be identified and consequently, the following separate sections have been presented:

a. developing an idea
b. organizing for action
c. establishing contact with funding source
d. writing a proposal
e. submitting the proposal and follow-up action
f. administering the grant

But the word "process" needs to be underscored. In large measure, success or failure in receiving funds from a funding source is determined by the thoroughness with which the various activities are undertaken and completed.

Additional Points

There is no guarantee that even with meticulous attention to details and to the sequential activities of the grantsmanship process, the outcome will be successful. There are a few points in addition to the material presented in the preceding chapters, however, which may increase the chances for securing external funds for a desired project.

In many of the cases where a grant is received, the grant administrator and the project director were involved throughout the process. Each, because of the focus of their eventual responsibilities, helped assure that the proposed project was realistic, was a part of the institution's mission and was feasible given the institution's resources and personnel.

In a similar manner, facility in implementing plans and success in achieving the goals and objectives of a funded project are often directly related to the lack of change in project personnel. When there is continuous involvement and continuity of personnel from one phase of the grantsmanship process to another, a kind of team spirit and commitment to the project is developed which aids in finding solutions to problems and unforeseen circumstances as well as in providing opportunities to discuss and eliminate individual frustrations and strains. The continued communication with, and involvement of, institutional staff members who are not project personnel helps insure that the institution's priorities and the goals and objectives of the project remain in harmony.

Included as a note of caution in the chapter on researching possible funding sources was the reminder of the adage "you don't get something for nothing." The acceptance of funds carries with it the commitment on the part of the grantee to fulfill some expectations of the grantor. Thus, it is initially important to make certain that the proposal clearly outlines the proposed activities and plan of action as well as defines the boundaries and constraints. The problem of clearly delimiting the project while at the same time keeping the proposal short and concise allows the possibility for the expectations of the institution and the expectations of the funding source to differ. Two-way communication preceding the submission of the proposal as well as possible communication during the review process will help decrease the possibility of incompatible expectations.

Executive Director of the Chicago Community Trust, Bruce Newman, offered additional helpful advice:

> It seems to me that one way of addressing the problem is to use appendices. Your primary proposal is short, but you provide the foundation executive with materials that make it possible to find out more about a problem if he or she wants to take the time to do so. That way you accomplish both. The decision can be made by the foundation staff person who is evaluating the proposal whether all the material needs to be passed along (to the board). We appreciate it when someone gives us background material we can use such as an article from a newspaper or magazine that describes a problem.[1]

---

[1]Timothy Saasta, "How Foundations Review Proposals and Make Grants—Part I," *The Grantsmanship Center News,* Nov.-Dec., 1976, p. 14.

Continuing contact and communication between the institution and the funding source are partially assured via the reports required in the grant agreement. But this type of contact is stilted and not conducive to establishing an enduring relationship. It is especially important to have other types of contact when the grant is the first one received from a particular funding source. Thus, the term that is more applicable to the whole spectrum of contact is not "communication" but, instead, "public relations."

Public Relations

The importance of public relations to the effectiveness of any institution is underscored by Harry Woodward, Luthern Resources Commission, in his emphatic statement, "A good public relations program is essential to a successful fund raising effort."[2]

Generally, the grantor encourages publicizing information about the funded project and making the results available to anyone interested. Public relations efforts often include news releases, articles, manuscripts, brochures, advertisments, still and motion pictures, speeches, association and professional meetings, symposia, etc. But whatever the public relations efforts, the sponsorship of the funding source should be acknowledged and, when possible, copies should be sent to the grantor and/or a representative of the funding source included.

The grant administrator and/or the project director also contribute to public relation efforts. In the course of carrying out their responsibilities of keeping informed on potential sources of funds, negotiating budgets and contracts and arranging site visits, relationships are established with foundation and agency representatives, auditors, officials monitoring the project and others who are interested in various aspects of the project activities and results.

To be most effective, the public relations efforts should be coordinated by one person. Even if there is a designated public relations person for the institution, most of the public relations function related to the grant will be coordinated by someone connected with the project, usually the project director or the grant

[2] "Guide to Public Relations for Nonprofit Organizations and Public Agencies," *The Grantsmanship Center News,* Jan.-March, 1977, p. 38.

administrator. But even though the function should be focused in one person, James Cossingham, Director of the Calhoun Community Action Agency, cautioned that everyone connected with the project should be aware of and involved in public relations, contributing ideas and effort. He stated, "One PR person, probably working part time, can't possibly carry a program. You get a multiplier effect if much time is spent helping the staff perform PR duties."[3]

Brian O'Connell in his book, *Effective Leadership in Voluntary Organizations*, further emphasized staff involvement. He observed that:

> One of the most important means of external communication starts with internal communications. If you keep your membership well informed, and particularly if you give them a feeling of the agency's activities and exciting thrust, they'll be telling the story by word of mouth.[4]

Thus, there are many dimensions of public relations which build interest in and support for a project in particular and the institution in general. For most institutions, the receipt of the first grant from a particular funding source is the beginning of what is hoped will be a continuing relationship beneficial to both the institution and the grantor. Consequently, public relations efforts should be aimed at creating confidence in the institution's capabilities and personnel and at establishing goodwill toward and support for the institution's mission.

Although the importance of public relations in the fund raising strategy is stressed, a tempering note should also be added, "Successful publicity does not make a successful organization. Too many organizations and personalities forget this. They begin to believe their own publicity."[5]

A Final Note

The above quote also can be interpreted to apply to the whole area of grantsmanship. The fact that carrying out the sequential activities resulted in the receipt of a grant should not cause a grantsman to become complacent and to expect to be successful

---

[3] *Ibid.*

[4] *Ibid.*

[5] *Ibid.*

every time. Competition for grant funds will continue to increase, both in terms of numbers and sophistication, and the successful grantsman will be the individual who continues to pay attention to details and who consciously works to develop and/or increase grantsmanship skills.

BIBLIOGRAPHY

Abarbanel, Karin. "Using the Grants Index to Plan a Funding Search," *Foundation News.* Vol. 17, No. 1 (January-February, 1976).

Allen, Herb, ed. *The Bread Game: The Realities of Foundation Fund Raising.* San Francisco: Glide Publications, 1974.

Baker, Keith. "The New Contractmanship," *The Grantsmanship Center News.* March-April, 1976.

Battle, Joseph; Melville, C. Bruce; Connell, Kenneth; Taffe, Donna; and Kramer, Ed. "How To Develop an Effective Fund-Raising Strategy," *Grantsmanship Center News.* August-October, 1976.

Beasley, Kenneth L. "Information Sources for Research Administrators," *Journal of the Society of Research Administrators.* Vol. VIII, No. 2 (Fall, 1976).

Belcher, Jane C. and Jacobsen, Julia M. *A Process for the Development of Ideas.* Washington, D. C: Government Relations Office, 1976.

Brodsky, Jane, ed. *Proposal Writers' Swipe File.* Washington, D. C: Taft Products, Inc., Non Profit Ability Series, 1976.

DeBakey, Lois. "The Persuasive Proposal," *Foundation News.* Vol. 18, No. 4 (July-August, 1977).

Federal Aid Planner: A Guide for School District Administrators. Arlington, Va: National School Public Relations Association, 1976.

Federal Funding Guide for Elementary and Secondary Education. Washington, D. C: Education Funding Research Council, 1974-75.

Flanagan, Joan. *The Grass Roots Fundraising Book: How to Raise Money in Your Community.* Chicago: The Swallow Press, 1977.

Funding Resources for Voluntary Programs. Richmond, Va: State Office on Volunteerism, Fouth Street Office Building, September, 1976.

Gansneder, Bruce M. "Program Evaluation," *Planning and Assess-*

ment in Community Education. Burbach, Harold J. and Decker, Larry E. eds. Midland, Michigan: Pendell Publishing Co., 1977.

Gold, Norman. "Preparing an Evaluation Proposal," *Proposal Development Handbook.* Baltimore, Md: Center for the Study of Volunteerism, University of Maryland, 1971.

Government Contracts and Grants for Research: A Guide for Colleges and Universities. Washington, D. C: Committee on Governmental Relations, National Association of College and University Business Officers, 1975.

Grants Administration Manual. Washington, D. C: HEW Department Staff Manual, 1976.

Hillman, Howard and Abarbanel, Karin. *The Art of Winning Foundation Grants.* New York: The Vanguard Press, Inc., 1975.

Improving Federal Grants Management. Washington, D. C: Advisory Commission on Intergovernmental Relations, February, 1977.

Jacquette, F. Lee and Jacquette, Barbara I. *What Makes a Good Proposal?* New York: The Foundation Center.

Jenkins, Patricia. "Guide to the New Grants Administration Standards for Non-Profits," *The Grantsmanship Center News.* November-December, 1976.

Lewis, Marianna O. ed. *The Foundation Directory.* New York: The Foundation Center, 1975.

Morgolin, Judith B. *About Foundations.* New York: The Foundation Center, 1975.

Pallante, James J.; McLaughlin, Gerald W.; and Smart, John C. "A Role Analysis of Higher Education Grant Administrators," *Journal of the Society of Research Administrators.* Vol. VI, No. 2,(Fall, 1974).

Proposal Development Handbook. Baltimore, Md: Center for the Study of Volunteerism, University of Maryland, 1971.

Putting It Together: A Guide to Proposal Development. Chicago: The Board of Education of the City of Chicago, 1975.

Saasta, Timothy. "How Foundations Review Proposals and Make Grants—Part I," *The Grantsmanship Center News.* November-December, 1976.

The Grantsmanship Workplan. Canoga, California: The Eckman Center, 1975.

Urgo, Louis. *A Manual for Obtaining Government Grants.* Boston: Robert J. Corcoran, 1970.

Utech, Ingrid. *Stalking the Large Green Giant: A Fund Raising Manual for Youth Serving Agencies.* Washington, D. C: National Youth Alternatives Project, 1976.

Williams, Walker A. and Company Inc. *Resource Development in the Private Sector: A Technical Assistance Manual.* Washington, D. C: Produced under contract administered by American Bicentennial Administration, 1976.

White, Virginia. *Grants: How to Find Out About Them and What to Do Next.* New York: Plenum Press, 1975.

Wilhelm, F. S. *A Manual of Policies and Procedures for Sponsored Research.* Eugene, Oregon: Office of Scientific and Scholarly Research, University of Oregon.

Willner, William and Hendricks, Perry B. Jr. *Grants Administration.* Washington, D. C: National Graduate University, 1972.

Willner, William and Nichols, John P. *Handbook of Grants and Contracts for Non Profit Organizations.* Woodward, Oklahoma: Bethesda Research Institute, 1976.

Zallen, Harold and Robl, Richard. *Planning for Research and Sponsored Programs: A Guide and Resource Book.* Stillwater, Oklahoma: Oklahoma State University, 1973.

Zallen, Harold and Zallen, Eugenia M. *Ideas Plus Dollars.* Norman, Oklahoma: Academic World Inc., 1976.

APPENDIX A

The Foundation Center:
National & Regional Collections

THE FOUNDATION CENTER

888 Seventh Avenue, New York, N. Y. 10019
Tel. (212) 489-8610
1001 Connecticut Avenue, N. W., Washington, D. C. 20036
Tel. (202) 331-1400

The Foundation Center was chartered in 1956 as an educational institution by the Board of Regents of the University of the State of New York. It is an independent agency, dedicated to the public interest and governed by its own board of trustees, usually half of whom are foundation officials and half public members from outside the foundation field.

The Center gathers and disseminates factual information on the philanthropic foundations through programs of library service, publication, and research. The Center's libraries in New York and Washington, D.C., contain extensive collections of books, documents, and reports on the foundation field and current files on the activities and program interests of more than 26,000 foundations in the United States. A national collection has also been established at the Donors' Forum, 208 South LaSalle Street, Chicago, Illinois 60604. In addition, The Foundation Center has established regional reference collections throughout the country where Center publications, as well as information on foundations in the immediate state or region, may be consulted. A list follows of regional collections, established as of the date this volume went to press.

NATIONAL COLLECTIONS

The Foundation Center
888 Seventh Avenue, New York, N. Y. 10019
The Foundation Center
1001 Connecticut Avenue, N.W., Washington, D.C. 20036
Donors' Forum
208 South LaSalle Street, Chicago, Illinois 60604

REGIONAL COLLECTIONS

Geographical Coverage

ALABAMA

Birmingham Public Library   Alabama
2020 Seventh Avenue, North
Birmingham 35203

ARKANSAS

Little Rock Public Library   Arkansas
Reference Department
700 Louisiana Street
Little Rock 72201

CALIFORNIA

University Research Library   Alaska, Arizona,
Reference Department   California, Colorado,
University of California   Hawaii, Nevada, Utah
Los Angeles 90024

San Francisco Public Library   Alaska, California, Utah,
Business Branch   Colorado, Montana,
530 Kearny Street   Hawaii, Idaho, Nevada,
San Francisco 94108   Oregon, Washington,
         Wyoming

COLORADO

Denver Public Library   Colorado
Sociology Division
1357 Broadway
Denver 80203

CONNECTICUT

Hartford Public Library   Connecticut,
Reference Department   Massachusetts,
500 Main Street   Rhode Island
Hartford 06103

FLORIDA

Miami-Dade Public Library   Florida
Florida Collection
One Biscayne Boulevard
Miami 33132

Jacksonville Public Library   Florida
Business, Science, and Industry Department
122 North Ocean Street
Jacksonville 32202

GEORGIA

Atlanta Public Library   Alabama, Georgia, Florida,
126 Carnegie Way, N. W.   Kentucky, Mississippi,
Atlanta 30303   North Carolina, South
                                                     Carolina, Virginia

HAWAII

Thomas Hale Hamilton Library   California, Hawaii,
Humanities and Social Sciences   Oregon, Washington
Reference
2550 The Mall
Honolulu 96822

IOWA

Des Moines Public Library   Iowa
100 Locust Street
Des Moines 50309

KANSAS

Topeka Public Library   Kansas
Adult Services Department
1515 West Tenth Street
Topeka 66604

KENTUCKY

Louisville Free Public Library   Kentucky
Fourth and York Streets
Louisville 40203

LOUISIANA

New Orleans Public Library   Louisiana
Business and Science Division
219 Loyola Avenue
New Orleans 70140

MAINE

Center for Research & Advanced Study   Maine
University of Maine at Portland-Gorham

246 Deering Avenue
Portland 04102

MARYLAND

Enoch Pratt Free Library Social Science and History Department 400 Cathedral Street Baltimore 21201	Maryland

MASSACHUSETTS

Associated Foundation of Greater Boston One Boston Place, Suite 948 Boston 02108	Connecticut, Maine, New Hampshire, Massachusetts, Rhode Island, Vermont
Boston Public Library Copley Square Boston 02117	Massachusetts

MICHIGAN

Henry Ford Centennial Library 15301 Michigan Avenue Dearborn 48126	Michigan
Grand Rapids Public Library Sociology and Education Department Library Plaza Grand Rapids 49502	Michigan

MINNESOTA

Minneapolis Public Library Sociology Department 300 Nicollet Mall Minneapolis 55401	Iowa, Minnesota, North Dakota, South Dakota

MISSISSIPPI

Jackson Metropolitan Library 301 North State Street Jackson 39201	Mississippi

MISSOURI

Kansas City Public Library 311 East 12th Street Kansas City 64106	Kansas, Missouri
The Danforth Foundation Library 222 South Central Avenue	Iowa, Kansas, Missouri, Nebraska

St. Louis 63105

NEBRASKA

Omaha Public Library   Nebraska
1823 Harney Street
Omaha 68102

NEW HAMPSHIRE

The New Hampshire Charitable Fund   New Hampshire
One South Street
Concord 03301

NEW JERSEY

New Jersey State Library   New Jersey
Reference Section
185 West State Street
Trenton 08625

NEW YORK

New York State Library   New York
State Education Department
Education Building
Albany 12224

Buffalo and Erie County   New York
Public Library
Lafayette Square
Buffalo 14203

Levittown Public Library   New York
Reference Department
One Bluegrass Lane
Levittown 11756

Rochester Public Library   New York
Business and Social Sciences Division
115 South Avenue
Rochester 14604

NORTH CAROLINA

William R. Perkins Library   North Carolina
Duke University
Durham 27706

OHIO

The Cleveland Foundation Library   Michigan, Ohio,

700 National City Bank Building Cleveland 44114	Pennsylvania, West Virginia

OKLAHOMA

Oklahoma City Community Foundation North Broadway Oklahoma City 73103	Oklahoma

OREGON

Library Association of Portland Education and Psychology Department 801 S.W. Tenth Avenue Portland 97205	Alaska, California, Hawaii, Oregon, Washington

PENNSYLVANIA

The Free Library of Philadelphia Logan Square Philadelphia 19103	Delaware, New Jersey, Pennsylvania
Hillman Library University of Pittsburgh Pittsburgh 15213	Pennsylvania

RHODE ISLAND

Providence Public Library Reference Department 150 Empire Street Providence 02903	Rhode Island

SOUTH CAROLINA

South Carolina State Library Reader Services Department 500 Senate Street Columbia 29211	South Carolina

TENNESSEE

Memphis Public Library 1850 Peabody Avenue Memphis 38104	Tennessee

TEXAS

The Hogg Foundation for Mental Health The University of Texas Austin 78712	Arkansas, Louisiana, New Mexico, Oklahoma, Texas

Dallas Public Library   Texas
History and Social Sciences Division
1954 Commerce Street
Dallas 75201

UTAH
Salt Lake City Public Library   Utah
Information and Adult Services
209 East Fifth Street
Salt Lake City 84111

VERMONT
State of Vermont   New Hampshire,
Department of Libraries   Vermont
Reference Services Unit
111 State Street
Montpelier 05602

VIRGINIA
Richmond Public Library   Virginia
Business, Science & Technology Department
101 East Franklin Street
Richmond 23219

WASHINGTON
Seattle Public Library   Washington
1000 Fourth Avenue
Seattle 98104

WEST VIRGINIA
Kanawha County Public Library   West Virginia
123 Capitol Street
Charleston 25301

WISCONSIN
Marquette University Memorial Library   Illinois, Indiana, Iowa,
1415 West Wisconsin Avenue   Michigan, Minnesota,
Milwaukee 53233   Ohio, Wisconsin

WYOMING
Laramie County Community College Library   Wyoming
1400 East College Drive
Cheyenne 82001

APPENDIX B

Federal Information Centers

ALABAMA

Birmingham
322-8591
Toll-free tieline to
Atlanta, Ga.

Mobile
438-1421
Toll-free tieline to
New Orleans, La.

ARIZONA

Phoenix
(602) 261-3313
Federal Building
230 North First Ave.
85025

Tucson
622-1511
Toll-free tieline to
Phoenix, Ariz.

CALIFORNIA

Los Angeles
(213) 688-3800
Federal Building
300 North Los Angeles St.
90012

Sacramento
(916) 440-3344
Federal Building and
U.S. Courthouse
650 Capitol Mall
95814

San Diego
(714) 293-6030
Federal Building
880 Front St.
92188

San Francisco
(415) 556-6600

Federal Building and
U. S. Courthouse
450 Golden Gate Ave.
94102

San Jose
275-7422
Toll-free tieline to
San Francisco, Calif.

COLORADO

Colorado Springs
471-9491
Toll-free tieline to
Denver, Colo.

Denver
(303) 837-3602
Federal Building
1961 Stout St.
80294

Pueblo
544-9523
Toll-free tieline to
Denver, Colo.

CONNECTICUT

Hartford
527-2617
Toll-free tieline to
New York, N. Y.

New Haven
624-4720
Toll-free tieline to
New York, N. Y.

DISTRICT OF COLUMBIA

Washington
(202) 755-8660
Seventh and D Sts., S.W.
Room 5716
20407

FLORIDA

Fort Lauderdale
522-8531
Toll-free tieline to
Miami, Fla.

Jacksonville
354-4756
Toll-free tieline to
St. Petersburg, Fla.

Miami
(305) 350-4155
Federal Building
51 Southwest First Ave.
33130

Orlando
422-1800
Toll-free tieline to
St. Petersburg, Fla.

St. Petersburg
(813) 893-3495
William C. Cramer
Federal Building
144 First Ave. South
33701

Tampa
229-7911
Toll-free tieline to
St. Petersburg, Fla.

West Palm Beach
833-7566
Toll-free tieline to
Miami, Fla.

GEORGIA

Atlanta
(404) 221-6891
Federal Building
275 Peachtree St., N. E.
30303

HAWAII

Honolulu
(808) 546-8620

U. S. Post Office
Courthouse and Customhouse
335 Merchant St.
96813

ILLINOIS

Chicago
(312) 353-4242
Everett McKinley Dirksen
Building
219 South Dearborn St.
60604

INDIANA

Indianapolis
(317) 269-7373
Federal Building
575 North Pennsylvania
46204

IOWA

Des Moines
282-9091
Toll-free tieline to
Omaha, Neb.

KANSAS

Topeka
295-2866
Toll-free tieline to
Kansas City, Mo.

Wichita
263-6931
Toll-free tieline to
Kansas City, Mo.

KENTUCKY

Louisville
(502) 582-6261
Federal Building
600 Federal Place
40202

LOUISIANA

New Orleans
(504) 589-6696
Federal Building
701 Loyola Ave.
Room 1210
70113

MARYLAND

Baltimore
(301) 962-4980
Federal Building
31 Hopkins Plaza
21201

MASSACHUSETTS

Boston
(617) 223-7121
J. F. K. Federal Building
Cambridge St.
Lobby, 1st Floor
02203

MICHIGAN

Detroit
(313) 226-7016
McNamara Federal Building
477 Michigan Ave.
48226

MINNESOTA

Minneapolis
(612) 725-2073
Federal Building and
U. S. Courthouse
11 South Fourth St.
55401

MISSOURI

Kansas City
(816) 374-2466
Federal Building
601 East Twelfth St.
64106

St. Joseph
233-8026
Toll-free tieline to
Kansas City, Mo.

St. Louis
(314) 425-4106
Federal Building
1520 Market St.
63103

NEBRASKA

Omaha
(402) 221-3353
Federal Building
U. S. Post Office
and Courthouse
215 North 17th St.
68102

NEW JERSEY

Newark
(201) 645-3600
Federal Building
970 Broad St.
07102

Trenton
396-4400
Toll-free tieline to
Newark, N. J.

NEW MEXICO

Albuquerque
(505) 766-3091
Federal Building and
U. S. Courthouse
500 Gold Ave., S. W.
87101

Santa Fe
983-7743
Toll-free tieline to
Albuquerque, N. Mex.

NEW YORK

Albany
463-4421
Toll-free tieline to
New York, N. Y.

Buffalo
(716) 842-5770
Federal Building
111 West Huron St.
14202

New York
(212) 264-4464
Federal Building
26 Federal Plaza
Lobby
10007

Rochester
546-5075
Toll-free tieline to
Buffalo, N. Y.

Syracuse
476-8545
Toll-free tieline to
Buffalo, N. Y.

NORTH CAROLINA

Charlotte
376-3600
Toll-free tieline to
Atlanta, Ga.

OHIO

Akron
375-5638
Toll-free tieline to
Cleveland, Ohio

Cincinnati
(513) 684-2801
Federal Building
550 Main St.
45202

Cleveland
(216) 522-4040
Federal Building

1240 East Ninth St.
44199

Columbus
221-1014
Toll-free tieline to
Cincinnati, Ohio

Dayton
223-7377
Toll-free tieline to
Cincinnati, Ohio

Toledo
241-3223
Toll-free tieline to
Cleveland, Ohio

OKLAHOMA

Oklahoma City
(405) 231-4868
U. S. Post Office and
Courthouse
201 Northwest 3rd St.
73102

Tulsa
584-4193
Toll-free tieline to
Oklahoma City, Okla.

OREGON

Portland
(503) 221-2222
Federal Building
1220 Southwest
Third Ave.
Portland, Ore.
97204

PENNSYLVANIA

Allentown/Bethlehem
821-7785
Toll-free tieline to
Philadelphia, Pa.   -

Philadelphia
(215) 597-7042

Federal Building
600 Arch St.
19106

Pittsburgh
(412) 644-3456
Federal Building
1000 Liberty Ave.
15222

Scranton
346-7081
Toll-free tieline to
Philadelphia, Pa.

RHODE ISLAND

Providence
331-5565
Toll-free tieline to
Boston, Mass.

TENNESSEE

Chattanooga
265-8231
Toll-free tieline to
Memphis, Tenn.

Memphis
(901) 521-3285
Clifford Davis Federal Building
167 North Main St.
38103

Nashville
242-5056
Toll-free tieline to
Memphis, Tenn.

TEXAS

Austin
472-5494
Toll-free tieline to
Houston, Tex.

Dallas
749 2131
Toll-free tieline to
Fort Worth, Tex.

Fort Worth
(817) 334-3624
Lanham Federal Building
819 Taylor St.
76102

Houston
(713) 226-5711
Federal Building & Courthouse
515 Rusk Ave.
77002

San Antonio
224-4471
Toll-free tieline to
Houston, Tex.

UTAH

Ogden
399-1347
Toll-free tieline to
Salt Lake City, Utah

Salt Lake City
(801) 524-5353
Federal Building
125 South State St. Lobby
84138

WASHINGTON

Seattle
(206) 442-0570
Federal Building
915 Second Ave.
98174

Tacoma
383-5230
Toll-free tieline
Seattle, Wash.

WISCONSIN

Milwaukee
271-2273
Toll-free tieline to
Chicago, Ill.

APPENDIX C
BASIC LIBRARY OF INFORMATION SOURCES
ACQUISTION ADDRESSES

Federal Register, Superintendent of Documents U. S. Government Printing Office, Washington, D. C. 20402.

Foundation Directory, Columbia University Press, 136 S. Broadway, Irvington, N. Y. 10533.

Catalog of Federal Domestic Assistance, Superintendent of Documents, U. S. Government Printing Office, Washington, D. C.

NIH Guide for Grants and Award Programs, National Institutes of Health, Division of Research Grants, Bethesda, Maryland 20014.

NSF Bulletin, Resource Office, National Science Foundation, Washington, D. C. 20550.

Humanities, National Endowment for Humanities, Washington, D. C. 20506.

Chronicle of Higher Education, 1717 Massachusetts Ave., N. W., Washington, D. C. 20036.

Federal Notes, Office of Federal Notes, University of Southern California, University Park, Los Angeles, Calif. 90007.

Commerce Business Daily, Superintendent of Documents, U. S. Government Printing Office, Washington, D. C. 20402.

Annual Register of Grant Support, Margis Who's Who, 4300 West 42nd St., Indianapolis, Indiana 46206.

U. S. Government Manual, Superintendent of Documents, U. S. Government Printing Office, Washington, D. C. 20402.

Higher Education and National Affairs, American Council on Education, One Dupont Circle, Washington, D. C. 20036.

SRA Journal, Society of Research Administrators, 2855 East Coast Highway, Suite 225, Corona del Mar, California 92625.

Science and Government Report, Northwest Station, Box 6226 A, Washington, D. C. 20015.

Commercial Clearing House—College and University Reports, 4025 W. Peterson Avenue, Chicago, Illinois 60845. Subscriptions include weekly issues, legislative dispatches, and two loose-leaf basic volumes; cost $625 for one-year subscriptions.

Government R & D Reports, MIT Station, P. O. Box 284, Cambridge, Massachusetts 02139; subscription $70 a year.

Federal Research Report, P. O. Box 1067, Silver Spring, Maryland 20910; semimonthly subscription, cost: $32.00 for one year.

ABOUT THE AUTHORS

Virginia A. Decker, M. B. A. and Larry E. Decker, Ph. D.

Although they have been residents of the Commonwealth of Virginia for the last five years and previously lived in several other states, Virginia and Larry Decker call Oregon "home." They each received Bachelor's and Master's degrees from the University of Oregon and they both began their personal education and experiences in the grantsmanship process in Oregon.

Virginia's exposure to the opportunities afforded by external funds began as an· assistant to one of her major professors who administered endowment funds. This initial experience broadened as she worked for both the Bureau of Business and Economic Research and the Bureau of Governmental Research at the University of Oregon.

Larry also began acquiring his grantsmanship experience while attending college. Upon completion of his Master's degree, he became the Director of the University of Oregon's Center for Leisure Studies and Community Service, which was established by a grant from the Higher Education Act of 1965, Title I. Under his guidance, the Center continued to receive awards of external funds and its reputation spread nationally.

Those initial experiences were followed by an internship with the Charles Stewart Mott Foundation as part of a doctoral fellowship at Michigan State University. Succeeding professional positions in the public school system of St. Louis Park, Minnesota and the University of Virginia also provided many opportunities to engage in the grantsmanship process.

For Virginia and Larry, grantsmanship has become a way of life. In a career that has taken them coast to coast, there have been many projects and activities supported by grants. Larry has served as a consultant for over 300 local, state and federal agencies, institutions and associations across the United States. The Deckers' experience includes writing and/or administering over 60 successfully funded proposals which total in excess of 5 million dollars. They also candidly admit that at least 10 non-funded proposals contributed significantly to their knowledge and experience.

Over the years, they have received increasing numbers of requests from aspiring grantsmen who ask, "Teach me how to get a grant." or "Help me write a proposal." The response to these appeals gradually grew into collecting and assembling materials on the grantsmanship process. The writing of *The Funding Process* came as the logical end product of their collection and assembly efforts.

★ ★ ★ ★ ★ ★ ★

Other Community Collaborators' Publications

The Basic Steps of Planning
by Ken M. Young

Creating Interagency Projects. . .
School and Community Agencies
by Joseph Ringers, Jr.

Community Involvement for Classroom Teachers
by Donna Hager, *et. al.*

For information, contact:

P. O. Box 5429
Charlottesville, Va. 22903

120